Manipulation and Body Language

Discover Emotional Manipulation Techniques and How to Analyze People

Erika Newton

Table of Contents

Manipulation

*Identifying Emotional Manipulation
Tactics and Dealing
with Manipulative People*

Declan Evans

Introduction

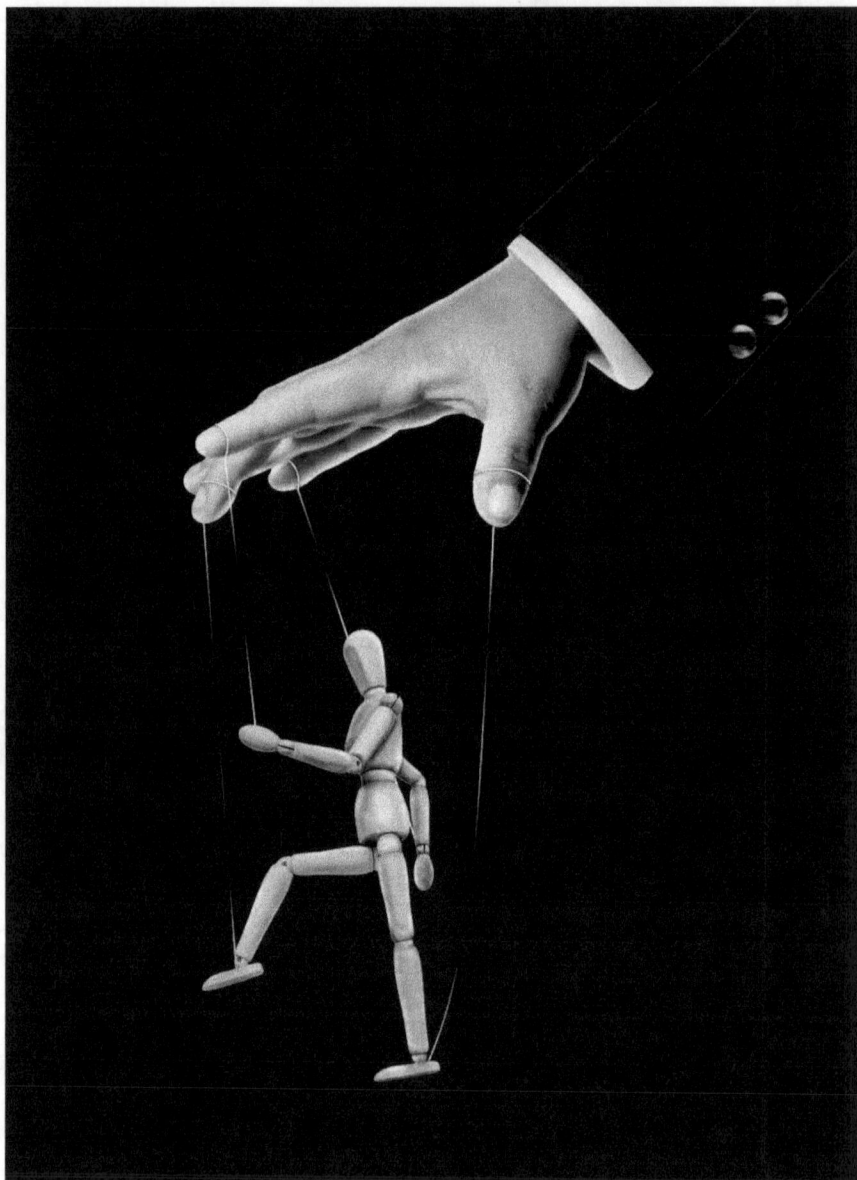

Manipulation has existed since the earliest civilizations. It is an ever-present yet background behavior that people use to benefit themselves. Usually, it is for the pettiest of reasons. But some have used manipulation for the attainment of great power such as the Roman emperors who manipulated millions, or today's politicians, who say what we want to hear. It even reaches down to lovers quarreling over their relationship.

This begs the question of why someone would use social subterfuge for anything. Well, looking at the people I mentioned above, they all have one thing in common. The power they wielded for the sake of power, and that power helped them accomplish many great things. Consider the modern corporate world. If you want to get ahead easily, you're going to do what is called "Playing the Game". Simply put, you act the way your superiors want you to act. In fact, you'd go out of your way to endear yourself to them. At the same time, you prove you are a more qualified employee for that opening you want to attain.

You manipulate but do not even realize it. Take, for example, the case where you are good friends with someone and have helped them with difficult tasks. Can manipulation be a good thing? So, now you need help moving, and you most likely call a close friend or family member because you know rather, subconsciously or consciously, that they will almost certainly help you.

Simply from prior interactions helping them, you'll both be amicable in helping one another. That is manipulation because you are recognizing that the individuals you are asking to help have asked you for help in the past. Hence, while this arrangement appears natural within the confines of the friendship, it is still a form of manipulation, nonetheless.

This is also the odd part of the manipulation. We use it so often in our daily lives to get what we want. We think it is a friendly tactic that benefits both parties so they both feel good in the end. We end up becoming oblivious to the insidious side of manipulation where the people use these tactics for no gain to the other. They just want us to be manipulated into believing what they are offering counts as some kind of gain.

All these behaviors are used in politics today. A famous book by an Italian, Niccolò Machiavelli, was written in Florence many hundreds of years ago. The simple premise is that it makes sense to manipulate since others would do the same to you had the tables been turned. His ideas help further cement these kinds of behaviors as normal and acceptable. And as a result, many despotic world leaders began to cling to them, believing it would provide them with power in the name of the people.

Concluding this point, some individuals who engage in manipulation are simply mentally ill, and as a result, their manipulative behavior stems from a place of hurt, because in a place of hurt, you are incapable of thinking rationally about your actions and the consequences that they may have on other people.

These people use emotional manipulation as a defense mechanism and, oftentimes, they do it because it is the only mechanism of psychological defense they know. Some intend no malicious harm nor are they mean at heart, but their behavior creates that appearance. They don't go out of their way to try to help others. Romantic manipulation is by far the worst yet most common form. It shatters trust and bonds. So, in future encounters with manipulators, you will remember these things, and they will help guide since you now understand their storied histories.

We can now look at manipulation as it occurs now in the 21st century. Most manipulation occurs in something as simple as social media. People manipulate and covertly trick us into thinking they live these blessed lives when, in reality, they don't. They show us only what looks good on the surface. In a way, manipulation has gone from the background to the foreground in our society. It has moved into our everyday lives with things like "fake news" and internet links designed to sound enticing yet simply accomplish nothing more than selling an ad.

You must understand how often manipulation occurs in this fast-paced world of ours. This may sound devious, but manipulation can also be used to accomplish great things that benefit everyone such as Gandhi's hunger strikes and other forms of peaceful negotiation. Just remember it has always been with us and will always be with us. It will just change form over time.

Knowledge is power and you, the reader, are now much better equipped to deal with manipulation when you encounter it. But heed these last words because when looking at the history of manipulation, do not always focus on the negative as sometimes manipulation has accomplished great things and has even saved lives has been the case in things such as diplomacy. Think of it this way: when you are arguing, it makes more sense to lie and tell them what they want to hear. If potentially millions of lives are at stake, then why would you want to risk anything for an absolute success. This may sound malevolent, but the fact of the matter is that sometimes a bit of dishonesty allows honest virtues to thrive.

Manipulation can also be used for good if you are a salesperson. The kind of manipulation used in sales tends not to be overt; it leans more on the subtle side of things because of the end goal. Remember while manipulation can look bad on the surface, the end goal is what truly matters.

So now that we have covered the basics of manipulation, you are probably left wondering why I mentioned that it can be used for good and may not always be bad. I will go into more depth on the matter to see the big issue of using manipulative tactics for good. There is the negative connotation the word manipulation carries when you hear it in reference to someone or an organization. You assume something nefarious.

This is simply false! Take the example of spies during World War II who helped defeat the Nazis. Their whole job was based on manipulation, but it was for a good cause – to save lives! The spies had to lie and play a part, while also manipulating a target to get exactly what they needed. The sad truth is that manipulation may in some situations be unavoidable – and we can't fool ourselves into thinking that good manipulation does not exist. Imagine you have bills to pay and you work at a car dealership. You need to sell cars, and we know that "sales tactics" are manipulation.

Sales tactics are used to create an emotional and economic incentive for a potential customer even though for the most part it's probably false. But in this case, both parties win. From the perspective of the car salesperson, they have now made a sale and can feed their families. From the customer's outlook, they now believe they have gotten a great deal on an expensive car and had somehow found someone to give them exactly what they want in a product, providing them with a sense of happiness. While on the surface, this is most definitely manipulation, it is something you could consider positive, given that both parties win in their minds.

There is importance in knowing when it's healthy to use manipulation to defend yourself. You suddenly start noticing your significant other always putting you on the spot, or playing the victim in every single situation.

Then it dawns on you they're a covert manipulator. Well if you know manipulation tactics, you can spot them in relationships and understand their use. You can completely avoid them, but chose to use your own manipulation out of peer necessity, such as to avoid harm. Oddly enough, using manipulation tactics against police officers to avoid a traffic stop is a good example. It is one of your choices, so you don't get hit with a big fine. If you play on emotions by claiming your violation for speeding was to visit a sick family member then, yes, it's outright manipulation although it saved you economically. I am sure this sounds bad but how many of us have found ourselves in a situation where we would do anything to get out of it. Well, sometimes when used right, manipulation is the best way to do just that.

Manipulation is part of human history

Looking at human history, we will see that some of our most loved historical figures practiced manipulation. During the formation of the United States, our founding fathers had to use socio-political manipulation to set a revolution in motion. First, they used various economical manipulation tactics on the other colonies such that colonists would join their cause and not that of the British. Second, many political games had to be played using subterfuge and manipulation to get the right people in place to lead the country.

Manipulation had to be used in its most persuasive form so the right person could get the right backing. This was not evil nor bad, as it showed how the covert tactic of playing into a willing pawn's card can allow everyone involved to win. Imagine, too, that they had to manipulate the British for quite a while before things truly were set in emotion. They had to manipulate them into trusting and believing them. These same manipulative games have been used for good by many great figures in history to manipulate the opposition into doing what is right.

Think of the rallies and marches during the civil rights movement that did so much good by playing on people's emotions and wants for a just society. This is not malicious manipulation, but just a necessary evil required to enact great change in this world.

Knowing that manipulation is not always an evil wantonly committed for its own sake makes it much easier to understand the tactics people use. A big part complimenting and persuading someone through one's charisma is in a sense manipulation. You are telling the person what they want to hear. Almost every friendship that is healthy uses such give and take. These are simple altruistic forms of manipulation that allow both sides to win and accomplish their goals Persuasion and charisma are the simplest forms of human manipulation.

Manipulators work by coming across as if they were a person who loves and cares and would drop anything if need be to help with something. This glib charm is a manipulative tactic that one uses to gain friends. Once again there is nothing wrong with this; it's in line with the gaming in the system. You are putting on a front that people want to see; and because of this, they become drawn to you and wish to spend their time with you.

This is the simple day-to-day manipulation that we all do – whether we realize it or not. On the social scale, it is not for harm, but companionship. Have you ever heard the expression "a little white lie?" It makes manipulation sound bad and evil. But the truth is that by doing the simple things characteristic of social charmer, like mirroring body language, buying food or goods, or always asking about the other's interests, while ignoring yours, is basic human interaction. You can get people to trust you and even help you get ahead in life through this kind of interaction in the social world.

Manipulation and success

You could argue that to a certain degree without some powerful people in society using manipulation to get their way to the top, the world would fall apart. Maybe we would not all be successful. This kind of manipulation is different than the more sinister version. Simply put, mental manipulation occurs during the nefarious act of playing mind games, such as making someone feel guilty for not buying or doing something, getting them to question their judgment.

This covert manipulative behavior has become so common that we oftentimes don't recognize it until it is too late at which point, we have to accept the consequences. Avoiding them is a great thing, but it can be hard if you are not sure what you are avoiding. That is why it is good to know what mental manipulation is despite its subtlety. It is perhaps the most common form of you will encounter in your day-to-day life.

Mental manipulation shows its face a lot in relationships with friends or other people you care about. As a result, those who do it are very good at it and hide it well. As said, it is a common form, but you must realize that there are many varieties of mental manipulation to which you could easily find yourself victim.

Consider the times when you were speaking with a group of friends and one person tried to make you feel guilty due to choosing not to buy them an extremely expensive gift for their birthday. They might try mental manipulation to get you to fall for the trap of, "oh well, I have done all these things for you, Don't you think it is fair if you get me XYZ".

Behavior like this is where manipulation becomes evil and unacceptable. This is not meant to sway someone over to your way of thinking for a good reason or trying to survive in a time of crisis. This narcissistic person is using manipulation to hurt another, and that is never acceptable.

Understanding the subtle moral differences in manipulation make it easier to learn about different manipulative tactics as a whole and how to go about defending yourself from them. It also gives you the ability to avoid people who could potentially manipulate you unknowingly, including the media and everything else we see. Since most use manipulation tactics, this is half the battle.

Chapter 1:
Character Traits of a Manipulator

Manipulation is a four-part process. By completing the four parts, you can manipulate anyone, easily. We are going to take a look at those four steps briefly and what is required at each step. Then, you will be walked through each step throughout the remainder of this book with specific instructions on how to effectively use them so you can easily manipulate anyone you chose.

Analyzing people

The first part of the process is to learn how to effectively analyze people. Before you can begin to manipulate anyone, you need to understand what techniques will work on them. Analyzing people may come naturally to you in many respects, but it will also require practice. Essentially, you want to get a grasp on who the person is and what drives them. For example, if they are heavily emotional, you will want to manipulate them using techniques that play on emotions. However, if you find that they are more logic-driven than emotion-driven, you will want to use techniques that play on their logical thinking side.

Analyzing people can be done in a few seconds, a few minutes, or even over several days or weeks. Naturally, the longer you have to do it, the more the chance you will successfully analyze them to successfully manipulate them. However, in many instances, and especially as you get better, you can easily analyze anyone in an instant and use this information to help guide you through the manipulation process. For example, if you are a salesperson, you may only have a few moments to properly analyze someone so you can sell something to them. In situations like this, you would need to be able to analyze said person very quickly. The more you practice, the faster you will get.

Manipulating people

Once you have successfully analyzed a person, it comes time to manipulate them. Manipulation is the part where you get to plant "seeds" in their mind to get them to agree with you on whatever it is that you want. Manipulation includes several tactics, often verbally-driven, that allow you to gain the acceptance of the "subject" at hand.

Ensure that manipulation comes after analysis, even if you only had only a few moments to analyze someone. Using the wrong manipulation tactics on the wrong person can result in them realizing what you are doing, thereby ruining your chance of success.

Manipulation is the entire purpose of this book, but it requires both analysis and persuasion to work effectively. For that reason, note that while this book will emphasize growing your ability to manipulate people, it will also focus heavily on how analysis and persuasion come into play with this practice.

Persuading people

Persuading people is the last step in the overall process of manipulation. This part of the process is often fueled by physical as opposed to verbal actions. These actions are an important part of manipulating people to agree with you or to comply with what you are asking for. You want to ensure that you are successfully using persuasion tactics to get your way every single time.

In this book, we are going to explore the most important persuasion tactics you need to know and when they should be used. This is essentially where you get to seal the deal and ensure that the outcome is in your favor. This will be the last active step in the 1-2-3 process you will use to manipulate people.

Staying secret about it all

The final part of the process is not necessarily a step like the previous three, but rather, it is a part you need to keep in mind the entire time you are manipulating someone. When you are practicing manipulation, understand that you must stay secretive about your intentions. If someone were to discover that you were manipulating them, two things would happen. First, that person would lose trust in you, ultimately taking away any chance you have at success in the future. Second, you would shed light on what you were trying to do, and they would see through every manipulation and persuasion tactic you try from thereafter. You must learn to stay completely secretive about your intentions throughout the entire manipulation process.

Manipulation is a practice that can be used by virtually anyone. There are no restrictions or limitations on who can use manipulation, or when. Naturally, you want to avoid using it at a time when it would be morally or lawfully wrong. For example, you would not want to manipulate someone into having a relationship with you when they do not want to, as this would not be correct. However, these strategies are phenomenal in business negotiations in trying to get what you want, by manipulating perceptions of who you are, among other things.

If you are interested in manipulating people, you must always start with one thing: coming across well before you even begin analyzing the person. That is, you should know exactly why you are manipulating the person. What are you trying to achieve with your manipulation strategies? What is your desired outcome? By having a clear understanding of what you are working toward, you will easily be able to choose the proper strategies to get there. Think of each of the techniques that you will learn about here as a vehicle to help get you where you want to go. All you have to do is pick the right one, and you will inevitably get there!

Chapter 2:
Types of Manipulation

According to research, there are three kinds of manipulation distinguished by the specific and particular intention of the manipulator:

Positive manipulation: where the aim of the manipulator is always right, useful, or pleasant for the person who is the object.

Egocentric manipulation: the manipulator turns the world around his interests, without worrying about the consequences for his victims.

Malicious manipulation: the intention of the manipulator, paranoid, conscious, and voluntary, is malice, or the destruction of others.

Positive manipulation: this manipulation is not always perceived as manipulation since its intention still appears to be good or pleasant. This is the case of a surprise for a friend or a gift to a child. This is also the case when a nurse says that everything will be okay before an injection, or a mother uses gentle persuasion to encourage her son to do his homework. "If you finish your homework this morning, you will have everything and the afternoon to do what you want. Otherwise, you will need to spend the day here without fun." Finally, it is also the case of an individual who seeks to show the positive aspects of something, which is a priori unpleasant. "I'm going to have to come home late tonight, I have to stay at the office...It's boring, but it will allow me to leave tomorrow at noon. That way we can go for the weekend earlier!" The manipulation is undeniable, but the intention always starts from the heart, so it is in no way to be condemned.

Egocentric manipulation: In this type, the manipulator thinks only of his interests, without worrying about others, nor about the discomfort that his behavior may generate. This manipulator will do everything to sell encyclopedias to the elderly, without worrying about their interests. This manipulator puts sticks in the wheels of his colleagues to make himself "well seen" by management or be promoted before them. The manipulator who makes all-out promises to get elected or the teacher who terrifies his class to establish his or her authority may not act out of spite and does not seek to harm anyone; but by thinking only of his interests, he inevitably harms others.

Marketers has become experts in this type of manipulation to get the customer to buy products. When they are offered a sample of pizza at the supermarket entrance, one in two will agree to taste it. But if the demonstrator touches their arms while making the tasting proposal, two out of three people will accept the offer and, above all, are twice as likely to put this same brand of pizza in their cart. (Extract from the Small Treatise on Manipulation for the use of Honest People by RV Joule and J. Beauvois)

Malicious manipulation
This last type is marked by the manipulator's conscious and voluntary attempt to destroy others. The goal is to ruin an individual somehow, maybe to damage an aspect of his personality, or otherwise harm his interests. It is a malicious and concealed intent.

Why are we vulnerable to manipulation?

It is not enough to know the definition of manipulation; it is still necessary to discover the reasons for our vulnerability to manipulation. Of course, they are multiple and different from one person to another. In general, the explanations stem from motivation and its two great strengths: the avoidance of suffering and the pursuit of pleasure.

So, a manipulative person can motivate you to do whatever they want because they strike a chord within you and cause discomfort or an emotion you don't want to feel. No one likes to suffer and feel guilt, fear, insecurity, helplessness, doubt, etc. So, you are being manipulated because you want to avoid suffering.

When your self-image is flawed - in other words, when you are unsure of yourself, of who you are and of what you want - manipulation can more easily cause you to doubt yourself and provoke guilt. For example, someone is sulking because you said or did something. To avoid guilt, you say that you didn't mean it rather than endure the sulking (a form of passive aggression). Example number 3 above is a good illustration of this.

Besides, manipulation tactics can also touch another of your fears, that of being judged. No one likes to be criticized for being selfish, incompetent, ungrateful, or inhuman. It could also be the fear of hurting, not being loved, losing an advantage, losing affection and respect, a material advantage, or even your job.

The manipulative person may control your behavior by giving you the hope of some sort of gain. It will make you expect. an emotional advantage, attention, recognition, status, even love, or a material advantage such as career advancement, reaching your goals more efficiently, obtaining results, and tangible rewards.

Here you are at the other great force of motivation: the search for pleasure. Of course, both types of motivation coexist in each of us, depending on the context. However, you probably have one strategy that takes precedence over the other, stemming from some sort of mental program that influences your actions no matter what decisions make. Some are more motivated by the stick and avoidance, while for others, it is the prospect of gain that motivates them to act. Recognizing this underlying tendency in yourself may help you understand how you come to be manipulated.

Recognizing a manipulator

Manipulation is the order of the day in today's world. It is done for power, by the media, and, of course, abounds in interpersonal relationships. In fact, with some frequency, we meet a master of manipulation frequently in our daily lives. Manipulation is a form of emotional blackmail. Certain behavior is set in motion to induce the other to think, feel, or act without realizing it, in the way the manipulator wants.

And that is precisely the significant problem of manipulation: it is covert behavior and not always detectable by those who fall victim to it. Hence, many take the bait and end up allowing the handlers to get away with it.

("The basic instrument for the manipulation of reality is the manipulation of words. If you can control the meaning of the words, you can control those who use those words." -Philip Dick)

Even if the manipulator hides under very different yet familiar traits, author Jacques Regard has identified a certain number of character traits that manipulators share. Here are the ways to identify a master of manipulation:

1. A manipulator make you feel guilty, and you don't know why: A master of manipulation consistently goes toward victimization. They likely have a "wild card trauma," that is, some problematic episode in their lives that they always expose as a justification for what they do maliciously. A "difficult childhood," "ungrateful children," "bad luck," and other common formulas are favorites. What reveals them is that they display emotional scars with some pride and the person even ends up bragging about them.

If, for example, you complain of a lack of consideration, they respond by saying something like "you get angry, but I had to put up with a father who abandoned me when I was three years old." Thus, they disarm you with their trauma. Who is going to be so insensitive as to complain to someone who has such a past? This is their game.

2. He threatens you without subtlety: Threatening indirectly is one of the recurrent tactics among manipulators. They have used it and continue to use it from great leaders to small domestic tyrants, while passing through seasoned publicists. This tactic consists of anticipating the worst possible outcome as a consequence of any of your behaviors.

"If you keep eating that way, in six months, you will be like a whale." They don't want you to eat, and they probably have no arguments to certify what they say; they just want you not to eat. Maybe they are bothered by how happy you are when you eat ice cream, or they think you spend too much money on food. They do not openly tell you what they believe, but merely pronounce.

3. He may disqualify what you do through sarcasm: If there's one thing a master manipulator hates, it's direct communication. "They don't name you a dog, but they offer you a bone," goes the famous saying. They often use sarcasm to ridicule you or downplay the value of your thoughts, feelings, or actions. The manipulator wants others to feel insecure and inferior.

An example of this is when someone sends you a seemingly friendly message that contains aggressive content: "Maybe if you read a little more, you could have better friends." Translated, it means: "You are an uneducated person, and that's why your friends are poor souls."

Sometimes, the manipulator's victim comes to believe that these insights are ways to help him be better. Nothing is falser. When someone wants to help another, use direct and honest communication. Also, it does not disqualify you but instead gives you a concrete contribution.

4. He is almost always charming: Typical handlers know that "the horse is stroked to mount it." They usually start their job by looking good and approachable. They fill you with compliments and show signs of exquisite taste, super-entertaining conversation, and high "sensitivity" to your expectations.

That is the first act. In the second act, things start to change. When they already have you convinced of how good they are, they go on to manipulate despite all that display of charm. They launch a kind of seduction network, and you are prevented from evaluating it objectively. You may see with good eyes what they are doing, and although doubts assail you from time to time, such that the person will always find a way to remind you that "you cannot think badly of someone who is truly fantastic."

5. *He becomes the judge of your life:* Without knowing it, suddenly the master of manipulation becomes a "spiritual guide" for your life. They are incredibly adept at telling others how they should live, even if they do not put into practice all that they proclaim. They give advice or expound great philosophical sayings. They tell you what to do, bit by bit. If it doesn't work out, they blame you. "I told you what to do; if you did not follow the instructions I so generously offered you, then it is your problem.

A good friend or a good counselor does not tell you what to do. Instead, he helps you discover it because everyone is different. the answer valid for "A" may not be valid for "B." as to who loves, wants you to be free and not dependent.

6. He is often imbued with excessive pride and tends to belittle others.

7. He regularly uses disinformation, lies, or slander.

8. He harasses insidiously by never intervening directly, preferring to push others to act in his place.

9. He always claims to work for a good cause and rarely admits his wrongs.

10. *He often speaks in a roundabout way*, never saying anything categorically, but sowing doubt in others' minds.

11. *He spreads rumors and conveys the worst calumnies without ever giving the impression of doing so*. He sometimes sends messages under the guise of frankness or awkwardness. He doesn't say anything, just repeats what he's heard or what the public rumor says.

12. *He is instantly outraged when we try to unmask him.* He takes neither his words nor his actions and turns everything to his advantage.

13. *He does not know how to listen to others' problems*, except when it allows him to achieve one of his goals.

14. *He devalues a lot*, often belittles and lies with incredible aplomb. He can contradict himself or disavow what he just said a few minutes before.

15. *He is good at speaking and at changing the subject:* Masters of manipulation are usually also masters of word art. They use flowery and glib speech. They always have a surprising or ingenious argument at hand, even if it is based on a lie. If they ridicule you, saying, for example, "In that dress, you look like a penguin," and you get upset, they will immediately add, "Sorry, I didn't think you were so sensitive to jokes." They always win. They are magicians at playing dumb. If you confront them, they divert the conversation to other topics, and when you least realize it, they are talking about matters that have nothing to do with what you initially started with.

16. *"Flip the cake" with ease:* "Flip the cake" means that they break the glass, but it is you who ends up paying for it and offering all kinds of excuses. A classic example of a master of manipulation is the husband who has been caught cheating. When his wife pulls out the motel bill found in his pocket, he becomes enraged and complains about her snooping through his personal belongings. He launches into a long spiel about the importance of trust in a relationship and respecting spaces. In the end, the woman feels so wrong that she ends up apologizing for being so "controlling," and the issue of infidelity ends up a misunderstanding that never should have occurred.

17. *He likes to surround himself with incompetent people at work:* By rewarding those who work poorly, he secures allies who are very devoted to him because, without him, they would be nothing.

18. He depletes the energy of those in contact with him.

Fundamental strategies against manipulation

The most basic and effective defense against manipulation is called reactance. In psychology, *reactance* is the natural reaction to rebelling when you realize that someone is trying to limit your freedom of choice. Because of reactance, a client does not want to be sold or want his friend to convince him of something he does not think to be true. That's why expert manipulators start their chess moves under the radar, so our reactance doesn't go off.

You cannot defend yourself from something you do not perceive, so the first step in protecting yourself from manipulation is to try to detect it. When someone perceives someone manipulating them, their reactance instinctively shoots up, and barriers are raised. In this way, we begin to deny false arguments, get defensive, and even dismiss things for our good.

Think of the rebellious teenager who ignores sound advice, or that customer who misses a real and valuable opportunity. It is reactance doing its part. People do not want to give up their freedom because that means that they lose status before the person who has imposed his will. The fundamental principle of manipulation is that the manipulator's real agenda remains hidden so that he does what he does to convince us "for our good."

But in the case of the manipulator, it is not for the sake reality. The fundamental difference between manipulation and persuasion is that the manipulator is only interested in profit and does not care what happens to others, so he will use tactics that persuasion does not apply, such as false information or emotions to the extreme. In practice, this implies that knowing more about manipulation and its mechanisms make us more immune to it. That is to say, the mere fact of reading this content will make you more resistant to being manipulated because you recognize the patterns and tricks used to deceive.

Here are the most effective strategies for self-defense against a manipulator:

Strategy 1: Asepsis and total avoidance

Do not get close to a handler; avoid contact and contagion as much as possible. Of all the strategies, this is the most effective. It's not the most epic, but it does work well. The first security strategy in any situation is always avoidance by all means. The basic strategy for winning a battle with a manipulator is not to enter I not the battle. That is the only correct maneuver because any other has consequences.

("A manipulator is an expert in fighting in the mud, from behind, and with low blows, he will win us if we go down to his ground.")

In bad times, both personal and business matters, there is the temptation to listen to dubious clients, frequently the worse companies. We may fall into "get rich quick" promises or "it's always someone else's fault" schemes. We have to avoid that as much as possible; we have to leave them alone and put a bell of silence on the manipulator.

It is far better to miss an "opportunity" to work with a manipulator than to get bogged down with one. Nobody goes around exposing themselves to the flu just to show how strong they are. Our primary strategy with any disease and with manipulation should be the same: do not enter their radius of action as much as possible.

Strategy 2: Cut the rope at once

The former is the best strategy, but it is impossible to avoid manipulation completely all the time. Sometimes, you will be caught off guard and circumstances will drag you into a situation, whether you like it or not. There will be times when it will be friends, family, or acquaintances involved in a manipulative situation and we may have to be involved.

("In these circumstances, and from experience, the appropriate strategy is to cut ties with the manipulator as soon as possible. We will do it quickly as if it were a clean blow of the sword. Then we take as much distance as possible.")

I know it may seem hard to be the vigilante and believe that we will not be fooled, but we must resist the temptation. Every minute you spend with a manipulator, you will be draining precious energy. The strategy is to disengage from the fight as soon as possible, "hit" only to gain distance, and then avoid further contact in the future.

If you are involved in business with a manipulator, terminate all contracts, say no to the slightest odd proposal, seek outside support, and do not isolate yourself by listening only to the manipulator.

Strategy 3: Never directly confront a manipulator

If you do, he will flee, play the victim, or use one of the many tricks in his hat. We have to be smarter than the manipulator.

("If you spot a manipulator, don't go straight for it, look for an indirect angle, and strike with one of the following strategies to break away from their influence and distance yourself.") I repeat, do not go to direct war.

Strategy 4: Never, absolutely never, lose your temper

As Americans say, business is business. This phrase alludes to a philosophy whereby there is no reason for emotions to get in the way of business. With the mentality of separating the professional from the personal, many businesses take some huge (business) wounds and solve them with, "It's just business."

("The exercise to be learned is that in business and against manipulation, you never lose your temper.")

If emotion surfaces, the manipulator wins. If he fails, he begins to despair, uses more violent tactics, exposes himself, makes mistakes, discovers his game, and loses the ability to manipulate. The manipulator seeks the brawl and that the other loses. We have to turn it around and use this strategy against him. We know we are winning every second that we do not lose our tempers and do not get carried away by emotion. Never get upset by a manipulator, be it a professional or personal situation. Use a surgical operation to remove it from your environment, and do not do more damage. He will twist, scream, and kick, getting louder and dirtier, like when little children get angry. But if we hold the guy to task, he loses.

Strategy 5: In business, get everything in writing

If the manipulator does not want to sign a contract, saying that "it is not necessary," and depends on trust, ignore it. ("Everything in business must be written and legal; in this way, we will close the doors to many manipulations, blackmail, and cheating.")

If a confrontation happens, we have evidence, and are in a perfect position under the law. If you have to fight to the last resort, pass the documents over to a lawyer and let him fight it out because it is his job. You dedicate yourself to growing your business and living your life.

Take a legal, robust position from the start. Thus, if you have to fight, it will not cost much to win. If you do not want to sign a document and want to keep it informal, you are not serious about business. That is why serious entrepreneurs sign everything in writing, it is the professional thing to do. Be protected lest something untoward arise.

A while ago, an excellent entrepreneurial friend found himself in the hands of a manipulative manager. It took a long time to cut the rope. He thought he could beat him when he had discovered the game (instead of walking away) and fell into the trap of trust that "no contract was necessary." It is always necessary.

The result was an economic hole of about eleven thousand euros in just a few months (we are talking about a relatively small business), thanks to funds the manipulator retained. He threatened to report my friend and wanted more money in exchange for dropping it. My friend could not prove that the other person was guilty of the theft of funds, although it was evident.

This is all 100% real and, sadly, typical. Before the showdown, he was calm and full of smiles; that's another typical manipulator trait. When things started to go wrong, he was an expert at blaming others, twisting the situation. Meanwhile, he kept collecting more money as there was no choice. A written contract (which this manipulator rejected from the start) would have solved everything.

Strategy 6: Learn to interpret signals

It is vital to recognize a manipulator and be aware of our emotional state in any negotiation, sale, or discussion with one. The four main clues that should set off alarms that we are in front of a professional liar are:

Insulation: Isolating ourselves in a conversation or situation is a sign of on-going manipulation. Isolation is a typical tactic that is used by cults. Any sensible person who proposes something to you should have no problem consulting other opinions.

Rush and pressure: When someone tries to get us to rashly buy a product, sign a contract, make any decision, or go out of business, something surely stinks. You have to distance yourself, consult other options, and decide what to do calmly. ("We should never make an important decision in a hurry or an upset, emotional state.")

Excess of emotions: Be careful when an excess of emotional is used in speech. Someone is likely trying to manipulate us. I have seen in person how individual, unethical companies in the field of self-help act, for example. They organize weekends where attendees are isolated in a hotel or spa; they are put in an altered and highly elevated emotional state (with exercises, practices, and speeches that strike a chord). It is all used to sell expensive programs and courses, in a rush, using pressure and a false shortage (another typical manipulation trick). ("If you put someone in a sufficiently upset emotional state, you can make them believe what you want.")

Excess "love" and attention: One of a cult's preferred strategies for attracting followers is called the "love bomb." It works because everyone accepts you unconditionally, smiles at you, and behaves like you are the best thing that ever happened to them, even though they hardly know you. There is no criticism; no one says no to anything; it is all gestures and acceptance smiles.

Acceptance is a harsh drug for anyone, but especially for those who have barely been able to obtain it, such as the lonely, the marginalized, or those going through a bad time. These people become scapegoats. We can all fall into the "love bomb" trap. There is a lack of seriousness, an excess of confidence, and often a refusal to sign contracts or agreements when everyone "is a friend"... All of these are signs of manipulation.

Strategy 7: In case of doubt about being a victim of manipulation, wait.

It is one thing for an offer to expire on day X, and another if the manipulator tells us it's now or never. Before someone asks us for a hasty yes or no, our tactic should never be to give an immediate answer. Like salespeople, who always have urgency, manipulators will try not to give us time to think because that is the only way the technique works. Use phrases to delay, such as, "What you are raising is very interesting and deserves some thought, " or "I'll keep it in mind and give you an answer later..."

Strategy 8: If in doubt, say you want to get a second opinion to see the manipulator's reaction.

Similar to the previous time strategy, in this case, we say we want a second opinion. Even when we are responsible for the decision to be made, we can always say that we must consult someone else: a lawyer, our spouse, or a friend who is an expert on the subject.

It is about trying to get out of the isolation trap with arguments that are difficult to refute. A desperate effort to prevent us from consulting a superior or an expert is a sign that we are being manipulated. These two strategies work as detectors for manipulators and differentiate them in a delicate situation.

Strategy 9: Do not give in to a manipulator or the most inoffensive details.

If you think you are dealing with a manipulator, don't say yes to anything no matter how innocent he seems. If we do, we are at risk of using cognitive dissonance (one of the fundamental principles of persuasion) to make us take a seemingly simple step to gradually give more agreement. When we realize it, it pushes us to the bottom of the well.

If you know you are involved with a manipulator, never get closer than necessary. Never say yes and never think you have everything under control. It must be noted that more often than not, we are not obliged to justify this refusal, as we are within our rights, and "no" is a complete sentence.

If he insists, we say the same no and do not add additional excuses that he can grab to counter attack. Manipulators are adept at emotional blackmail and getting those excuses to turn them around.

Strategy 10: Be very clear about the initial objective you have in mind.

This is the first golden rule of negotiation, but it should be remembered in any situation in which we interact with a manipulator.

("If your objective in the conversation or negotiation with a manipulator is vague and diffuse, you will end up at the point that the manipulator wants.")

Be very clear about what you want. Never confront a manipulator without knowing precisely what you want to get out of the interaction. If you're going to cut ties with the manipulator, focus on reducing the links. If you want to hear what he has to say and then reflect, with other opinions and without pressure, keep that in mind and don't allow anything else to happen.

Listen and then don't let the manipulator talk about anything other than the goal you have in mind. Since this is the real world, you should have an ideal target in mind and then a realistic goal. Be prepared to compromise (though not too quickly) from that ideal goal to the actual one. That is the minimum limit so do not make another step. Know your destiny, as far as you can give in, and then do as Ulysses did when returning from Troy. Hold on tight to your targets and resist any manipulative siren calls.

Strategy 11: Never use the same weapons as the manipulator.

There is a powerful temptation to use weapons of manipulation against a manipulator. To respond with fallacies, try to isolate him, do emotional blackmail, or put on an act to increase the emotion in the situation is wrong.

("Don't fall for it, because they are based on lies, which has practical consequences. I do not want to sound like a preacher, but they never come out for free.")

There is a red line that delimits persuasion and manipulation techniques. The first few times, this line commands respect, and it is difficult to cross it. But when we've crossed it and have fallen into unethical manipulation, the line is blurred even for a legitimate purpose. That way, it is much easier to transfer it again a second time. Do it a few more times, and the line will be erased, and we will have become one of them.

But it is also a fact that manipulation is not necessary. There is a large amount of material on ethical persuasion; you can use scarcity without isolating or pressing, and you can use cognitive dissonance without it being a trap to fleece a victim. Always remember to have ethics, because if there is one thing I have learned it is that manipulators do not end well.

Chapter 3:
What is Covert Emotional Manipulation?

Covert emotional manipulation is used by people who want to gain power or control by deploying tactics that are both deceptive and underhanded. Such people want to change the way you think and behave without you ever realizing what they are doing. In other words, they use techniques that can alter your perceptions in such a way that you think you are doing it out of your own free will. Such emotional manipulation is "covert" because it works without you being consciously aware of it. People who are good at deploying such techniques can get you to do their bidding without your knowledge; they can hold you "psychologically captive."

When skilled manipulators set their sights on you, they can get you to grant them power over your emotional well-being and even your self-worth. They will put you under their spell without you even realizing it. They will win your trust, and you will start attaching value to what they think of you. Once you have let them into your life, they will then start chipping away at your very identity in a methodical way; and as time goes by, you will lose your self-esteem and turn into whatever they want you to be.

Covert emotional manipulation is more common than you might think. Since it's subtle, people are rarely aware that it's happening, and in many cases, they may never even notice. Only keen outside observers may be able to tell when this form of manipulation is going on.

You might know someone who used to be fun and jovial, then she got into a relationship with someone, and a few years down the line, she seems to have a completely different personality. If it's an old friend, you might not even recognize the person she has become. That is how powerful covert emotional manipulation can be. It can completely overhaul someone's personality without them even realizing it. The manipulator will chip away at you little by little, and you will accept minute changes that fly under the radar, until the old you is replaced by a different version, build to be subservient to the manipulator.

Covert emotional manipulation works like a slow-moving coup. It requires you to make small progressive concessions to the person trying to manipulate you. In other words, you let go of tiny aspects of your identity to accommodate the manipulative person, so it never registers in your mind that there is something bigger at play.

When the manipulative person pushes you to change in small ways, you will comply because you don't want to "sweat the small stuff." However, there is a domino effect that occurs as you start conceding. You will be more comfortable making subsequent concessions, and your personality will be erased and replaced in a cumulative progression.

Covert emotional manipulation occurs to some extent in all social dynamics. Let's look at how it plays out in romantic relationships, in friendships, and at work.

Emotional manipulation in relationships

There is a lot of emotional manipulation that takes place in romantic relationships, and it's not always malicious. For example, women try to modify men's behavior to make them more "housebroken"; that is just normal. However, there are certain instances where the person's intention is malicious, and he/she is motivated by the need to control or dominate the other person.

Positive reinforcement is perhaps the most used covert manipulation technique in romantic relationships. Your partner can get you to do what he wants by praising you, flattering you, giving you attention, offering gifts, and acting affectionately.

Even the seemingly nice things in relationships can turn out to be covert manipulation tools. For instance, your girlfriend could use intense sex as a weapon to reinforce a certain kind of behavior in you. Similarly, men use charm, appreciation, or gifts to reinforce certain behaviors in the women they are dating.

Some sophisticated manipulators use what psychologists call "intermittent positive reinforcement" to gain control over their partners. The way it works is that the perpetrator will shower the victim with intense positive reinforcement for a certain period, then switch to just giving normal levels of attention and appreciation. After a random interval of time, he will again go back to the intense positive reinforcement. When the victim gets used to the special treatment, it's taken away, and when she gets used to normal treatment, the special treatment is brought back, and it all seems arbitrary. Now, the victim will get to a place where she becomes sort of "addicted" to the special treatment, but she has no idea how to get it, so she starts doing whatever the perpetrator wants in the hope that one of the things she does will bring back the intense positive reinforcement. In other words, she effectively becomes subservient to the perpetrator.

Negative reinforcement techniques are also used in relationships to manipulate others covertly. For example, partners can withhold sex as a way of compelling the other person to modify their behavior in a specific way. People also use techniques such as silent treatment and withholding of love and affection.

Some malicious people create a false sense of intimacy by pretending to open up. They share personal stories and talk about their hopes and fears. When they do this, they create the impression that they trust you, but their intention may be to get you to feel a sense of obligation towards them.

Manipulators also use well-calculated insinuations to get you to react in a certain way at the moment, to modify your behavior in the long run. Such insinuations can be made through words or even actions. In colloquial terms, we call this "dropping a hint." People in relationships are always trying to figure out what the other person wants out of the relationship, so a manipulative person can drop hints to get you to do what they want without ever having to take responsibility for the actions you take because they can always argue that you misinterpreted what they meant.

Dropping hints isn't always malicious (for example, if your girlfriend wants you to propose, she may leave bridal magazines out on the table). However, malicious insinuations can be very hurtful, and they can chip away at your self-esteem. Your partner can use insinuations to suggest you are gaining weight, you aren't making enough money, or even that your cooking skills aren't any good. People use insinuations to get away with "saying without saying," any number of hurtful things that could affect your self-esteem.

Emotional manipulations in friendships
Covert emotional manipulation is quite common in friendships and casual relationships. Friendships tend to progress slower than romantic relationships, but that just means that it can take a lot more time to figure out if your friends are manipulative. Manipulation in friendships can be confusing because even well-meaning friends can come across as malicious. That's because there is a certain social rivalry that exists between even the closest of friends, which explains the concept of "frenemies."

Manipulative friends tend to be passive-aggressive. This is where they manipulate you into doing what they want by involving mutual friends rather than coming to you directly. Passive aggression works as a manipulation technique because it denies you the chance of directly addressing whatever issue your friend is raising, and so, in a manner of speaking, you lose by default.

For example, if a friend wants you to do her a favor, instead of coming out and asking you, she goes to a mutual friend and suggests she ask you on her behalf. Now, when the mutual friend approaches you, it becomes very difficult for you to turn down the request because there is added social pressure. When you say no, your whole social circle now perceives you as selfish.

Passive aggression can also involve the use of silent treatment to get you to comply with a request. Imagine a situation where one of your friends talks to everyone else but you. It's going to be incredibly awkward for you, and everyone will start prying, wondering what the issue is between the two of you, thereby taking sides on the matter.

Friends can also covertly manipulate you with subtle insults. They can give you back-handed compliments that have hidden meanings. When you take the time to think about what they meant by the compliment, you will realize that it's an insult in disguise that will bruise your self-esteem and possibly modify your behavior.

Some friends will manipulate you by going on a "power trip" and trying to control your social interactions. For example, there are those friends who are going to insist that every time you hang out, it should be in their apartment or at a social venue of their choosing. Such friends often have the intention of dominating the friendship, so they are keen to always have the "home ground advantage" over you. They'll try to push you out of your comfort zone, just so you reveal your weaknesses and then become more emotionally reliant on them.

Manipulative friends tend to excessively capitalize on your friendship, and do so to a disproportionate degree. They will ask for lots of favors with no regard for your time or effort. They are the kinds of friends who will leverage your friendship every time they need something, but then they make excuses when it's their turn to reciprocate.

Emotional manipulation at work

There are many reasons why a colleague might want to manipulate you. It could be you are on the same career path, and so he wants to make you look bad. It could be that he is lazy and wants to stick you with his responsibilities. It could also be that he is a sadist and just wants to see you suffer.

One way people at work exert their dominance over others is by stressing them out and then almost immediately relieve the stress. Say, for example, you make a minor error on a report, and your boss calls you into his office. He makes a big fuss and threatens to fire you, but then towards the end, he switches gears and reassures you that your job is secure as long as you do what he wants. That kind of manipulation works on people because it makes them afraid and gives them a sense of obligation at the same time.

Some colleagues manipulate you by doing you small favors, and then reminding you of those favors every time they want something from you. For instance, if you made an error at work and a colleague covered for you, he may hold it over your head for months or even years to come, and he is going to guilt you into feeling indebted to him.

Colleagues can also manipulate you by leaving you out of the loop when they are passing across important information. The intention here is to get you to mess up so they can have a better standing with the boss or other colleagues. When you discover that someone is leaving you out of the loop at work and you confront them, they may feign innocence and pretend that it was a genuine mistake on their part, or they could find a way to turn it around and blame you.

People with dark personality traits tend to be hyper-competitive at work, and they won't hesitate to use underhanded means to pull one over on you. Most colleagues turn out to be good friends, but you should be careful with those overly eager to befriend you. It could be that they want to learn more about you so that they can figure out your strengths and weaknesses, and find ways to use them against you. Narcissists, Machiavellians, and psychopaths are very good at scheming at work, so don't let them catch you off guard.

Chapter 4:
Manipulation and Emotional Exploitation

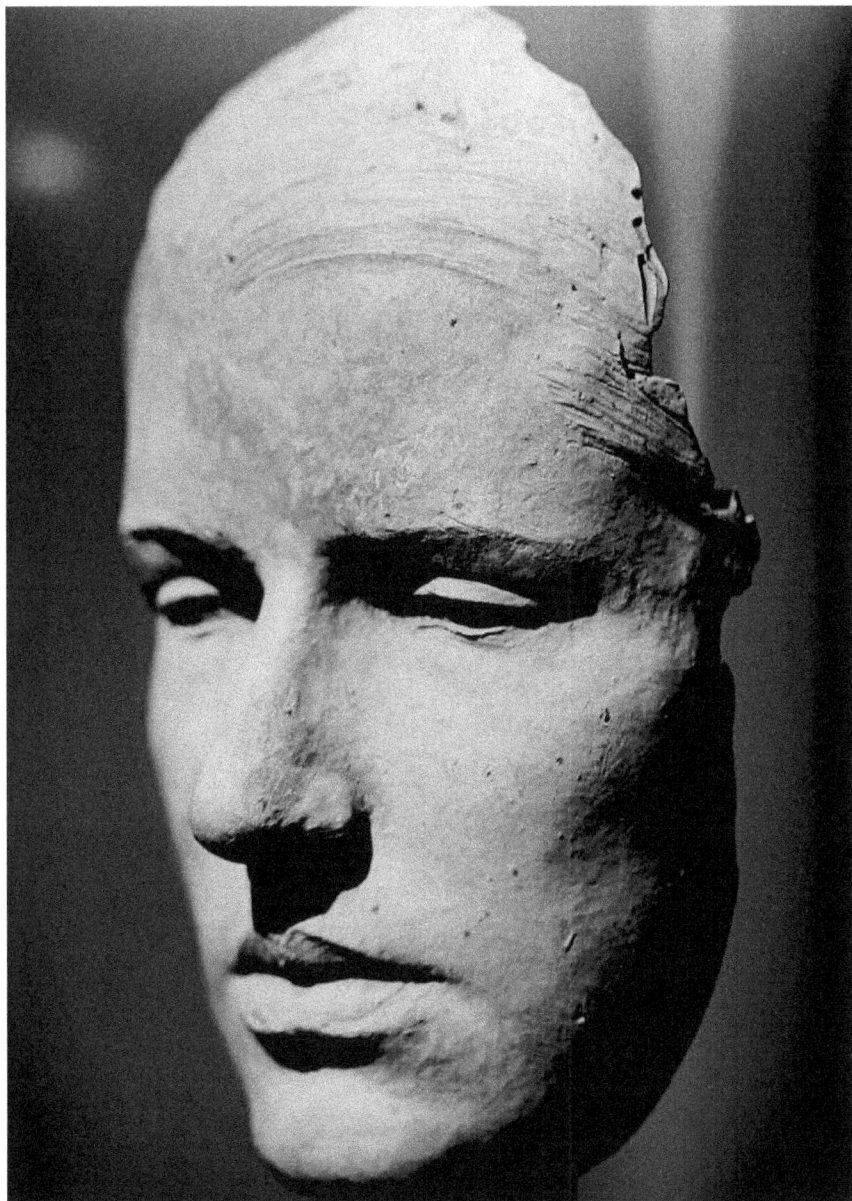

Why me?

Why do some people get taken advantage of and others don't? It seems like a crap-shoot, I know. But it's not. Everything happens for a reason. If you're gullible, chances are there is something in your upbringing that made you that way. If you seek approval at all costs, chances are it sems from something in your childhood. As sad as it is, what happens to us in our younger years does more to shape us than anything else.

Some children are nurtured. They have stable families with no traumatic upheavals. They seem to have it all together. Here's the deal; no one has it all together. But some have it more together than others.

If you're frequently the victim of manipulation, then you need this book. You've got to learn to watch for signs of it whenever you're dealing with authority figures. You may not fall for it from everyone, but you might have a harder time seeing it in people you're supposed to trust: your boss, your kids, and even your spouse. If people are often trying to sway you to their way of thinking or doing things for them that they should be doing themselves, then you should be doing a better job at watching out.

Here's an example of a person who is being manipulated or emotionally exploited: Jane goes to work each day. She wants to do a great job and please her boss at all costs. One day, Jane is feeling ill. She has a terrible headache and calls in to ask her boss for the day off. He tells her he can't spare her today, saying just come in and do your best.

Sounds reasonable, doesn't it? Only when Jane gets into work, she finds two extra people who've been scheduled to work too. They're overstaffed. So, she goes in to tell her boss that she is still feeling terrible and since the place is overstaffed, can she please have the day off. She understands she's giving up the pay for the day.

Still, he says he needs her. She's a great worker. Sorry, she can't leave. And as a matter of fact, she needs to go scrape all the gum off the salesroom floor, and after that, the toilets need a good scrubbing. And then he needs her to drive downtown to pick up his lunch. He's a diabetic, and this is the only place that has those sugarless twinkies he loves so much. It's his one treat for the entire day; he **so** needs it.

Jane doesn't do what someone who refuses to be emotionally exploited does. She bows her head, tells him she'll do it all, and even thanks him before leaving his office. She could've handled things very differently. She could've done things in a way that would've made her boss see that she wasn't a person who could be taken advantage of or manipulated. With just a few words said differently, she could've stayed home and taken care of herself.

These words are simple and, unfortunately, people with the affinity to be emotionally exploited use them far too sparingly.

Here they are **the magic words**: I'm sick, I won't be coming in today. (There is absolutely no reason to ask a question here. You are sick, and you won't be in – end of subject) When asked to do something you feel uncomfortable doing, unsafe doing, or that is not your responsibility, here is what you say: No. I will not do that.

When asked why you won't be doing it, here's the magic answer: Because I do not want to. Now, if you've been giving in to this person for some time, you can expect some negative feedback. They do think they can manipulate you after all. Don't let them say too much. Cut them off with some quick words of your own. Such as, you have my answer, goodbye.

It takes practice but staying true to yourself over anyone else is important, and you can do it. The way I think about it is like this. If I'm sick and someone wants to keep pushing me to work anyway, I ask myself, would you die for this SOB? Usually, my answer is no. Now, when it's a helpless little kid or a helpless elderly person, I suck it up and do what needs to be done. Other than that, it can wait, or someone else who isn't feeling sick can do it.

Here are some ways people can manipulate you or emotionally exploit you and how to handle each situation:

Love flooding

This is when someone is buttering you up to get you to do something they know you don't want to do. They may come and lather you with affection like sweet kisses, hugs, nuzzle. "Baby, I love you. Can you get up and do my laundry quick so I can stay in bed and sleep?"

Normally, you might be nice and do it. But last night, you were up with the baby six times. And you've got an appointment with the dentist that you're not looking forward to after lunch. You don't want to get up and even start your day, much less someone else's – even if you truly love that other person.

Here is how you handle this sweet talk but still know that it's a manipulation: "I love you, but our child kept me up, and I'm not looking forward to my day as it is, so no. You're on your own with your laundry, and as much as I love your affection, I'm not looking for any at this moment. I need my sleep. Night-night."

Lying

Most people can't abide liars – I'm one of those people. I will bend over backward for you, but if I catch you lying to me, then that's over and quick.

Lying happens a lot when someone wants you to give them some money. Here's an example and how you handle it without getting duped.

"I hate to ask, but I don't have a dime to my name, and little Susie has a terrible cold. The medicine is only ten bucks, but I don't have it. If I don't get some money, she'll suffer all night. And I don't get paid until Friday – that's three days away. I'm just worried about Susie is all, or I wouldn't even ask to borrow twenty bucks."

"I thought the medicine was ten dollars?"

"Yeah, it is. But while I'm out, I thought I'd pick up something to eat. You know, hamburgers, fries, a soda or two. Poor Susie is dying for her favorite junk food too. Poor baby."

All of a sudden, you see little Susie running around behind her momma's back, jumping off the furniture, laughing her head off. Now is your chance to do what's right. So, you say, "She looks fine to me. I would've bought that child's medicine had she been sick. Don't ask me for money anymore." Then walk away without looking back.

Withdrawal

This is a hard one. When someone gives you the cold shoulder or shuts themselves off just because you won't do what they want, then it hurts. I don't care who you are or how tough you might be. When someone turns away from you only because you won't do what they want, it's terrible manipulation and the epitome of emotional exploitation.

It's easy to say, "Just don't let them get to you, but man, that's right at impossible." That is until you realize why they're doing it. They want you to feel terrible for not giving in to them. They want to make you hurt. And for what?

Most of the time, what they wanted doesn't amount to a hill of beans. Here's an example and how you should handle it:

You come into the living room, your arms full of groceries that you need to unpack and put away. Your mother is sitting in the living room, doing her nails. "Can you run out and feed my dogs, real quick?" she asks.

"I can't, Momma. I've got to put these groceries away, and I've got another armload in the car, then I've got to get to the school to pick up Ariel and get her to the doctor to get those warts of hers frozen off. Sorry."

"My nails are wet. I wouldn't ask you if it wasn't important."

'I'm sure your dogs won't die before your nails dry, and you can get out there to feed them. Momma. I am in a huge rush right now.'

"It's just a small favor. You're being selfish. The dogfood is right there by the backdoor. You're right there by it. Now, put one scoop in pen for Fancy and then get a scoop out of the other bag for Bossy, he can't eat what Fancy does."

"Mom, I know what they eat and how they eat it. I just don't have time right now. If you don't want to go outside, I'll feed them as soon as I get back home."

The bottle of nail polish goes flying. Nothing but the sound of stomping is heard as the room is vacated. The sound of a door slamming is the last thing you hear. It's not the first time this has happened, and you know it won't be the last. What do you do? The last time she got mad like this, it was three days before she said one word to you?

I've lived this. I've dealt with this over and over in my life. My mother was one person who did this to me and my husband the other. I never learned how to deal with my mother, but you can bet I wasn't going to deal with this from my husband. So, I learned how to handle people who try to manipulate me by using this tactic.

Calmly, you go to where they've shut themselves off from you. You don't have to open the door; just speak calmly through it. "You're upset, that's plain to see. I am busy. That is also plain to see. You can pout, you can keep your distance from me, and you can keep your words to yourself too. You aren't hurting me if that's what you were going for. You're hurting yourself. You deny yourself human interaction." And then you walk away. You don't go do what she wanted you to do. You go on about your business, and if she's still not talking when you get back, you reiterate to yourself that she is only hurting herself, and you can't be hurt by that.

Love denial

Much like withdrawal, love denial is when a person who loves you holds back attention because you won't do something they want you to. You can use the same type of scenario from above to deal with that person. You will still talk calmly and let them know that what they are doing is only hurting them and not you. They are the ones who are missing out on love and attention by acting the way they are. You have to stay strong here and remain calm. They have learned this. It was done to them. Have empathy for that, but don't tolerate it. Don't give in to it. They will learn that at least you won't be manipulated by this action.

Choice restriction

Many of us have done this with our children. We offer only the choices we want them to take while ignoring the ones we know they want. For instance, little Sally is looking at the candy bars in the grocery store. We hold up grapes and apples. "Sally, you get to pick the treat today. Is it going to be apples or grapes?"
With only the two things to pick from, she's stuck.
But that's a child, and you're doing it for good purposes, not evil ones. Now you're a grown person and you want to eat Chinese food for lunch. You and your sister are in the food court at the mall and there are tons of choices. So, it stuns you when your sister says, "Oh, I don't want Chinese today. I'll let you pick though – pizza or burgers? Go ahead. You get to pick."
I'm pretty sure there aren't lots of you who even need to know what to say here, but I'll put it out there, just in case.
You say, "Get a grip, sis. I'm getting Chinese. You get whatever the heck you want."

Reverse psychology

Again, many of us have used this method of manipulation on our children and even grown individuals to get them to see things our way. You want your kid to put on their protective shoe coverings to go out into the rain. You know that your son hates to be told what to do. So, you say, "It's pouring out, but I don't see any reason for you to put your galoshes on over your new shoes. They should be fine."
"I don't want my shoes to get ruined, Mom. Gee whiz! I'm wearing them today."
You smile, mission accomplished. But what if it's happening to you? Your hubby would like his favorite shirt washed but doesn't want to do it himself. He says, "Aw, man. My favorite red shirt is dirty." He grabs up the red shirt and a handful of other clothes out of the hamper. Your white shorts and blouse are in the mix. "I'll just do a load. Don't worry, babe. I've got this."

you might be overlooking the obvious. He's hoping you will see the whites and stop him, take over, do the load yourself. But you see what he's doing and stop him. "Oh, here let me take those whites. No reason for you to wash these with that red shirt, as it'll turn them pink. There you go. You're good to go now, babe."

He's left frowning as his ploy did not work and you walk away with a smile on your face.

Semantic manipulation

This one is pure torture. I am positive that you've said or have been told, "I'm not going to argue semantics with you." This is when someone wants to use your words, turn them into pretzels, and do their level best to drive you insane.

Think about any argument you've ever had with a child over doing their homework. "But I thought the teacher meant next Tuesday, not today. Why would they expect me to turn it in with only one night to finish it?"

"Um, because it's only three lousy questions that would've only taken you ten minutes to finish."

You're out of your mind, and they're still trying to tell you what they thought. Although it's nearly impossible to shut this type of thing down quickly, you must try. A calm voice never fails to get someone's attention. "Well, you were wrong about that. So, here it is in nice simple language for you. Do the questions now." Then walk away without saying another word. Don't listen to the rubbish that will surely pour from their lips, just keep on walking.

My best advice when you are faced with any type of manipulation at all is to walk away. Sometimes, there are no words that will get through to the person. Sometimes, you must just remove yourself from the equation.

If words are a thing you find necessary, say them with a calm tone, but make it short and concise and do not expect an answer. Walk away. Leave them on their own to think about what you said or did not say. Most of all, remember that this is **their** problem, not **yours**. Don't let it become your problem.

DIY exercises

You're busy at work, doing end-of-the-month reports only you can do, when your boss comes in and tells you to put that to side for now. He needs you to run an errand for him. You can take the reports home to finish them on your own time. What do you tell him?

_____
_____
_____
_____
_____
_____

After you tell your husband that you can't stop what you're doing to cut his toenails at that minute, he storms out. What do you do?

Chapter 5:
Social Manipulation Strategies

Learning about mind control is most effective when you get an idea of what it truly looks like in action. This will ensure that you are right in your beliefs about how each technique should look and you are prepared to use it in real-life scenarios. The following three samples will teach you exactly what mind control strategies should look like in action. This will help you become masterful at using mind control on people.

Scenario one: making a sale

One situation where you may want to exercise your brainwashing abilities is making a sale in your business. With the modern world being taken over by new entrepreneurs, it can be easy to feel like you might be one of the few who struggle with sales. You can certainly change the face of this experience by learning how to use brainwashing to get people to purchase products from you.

Imagine the following scenario between Margaret (the buyer) and Darren (the seller). This will get an idea of what mind control looks like in a real life situation.

Margaret: "What an interesting product. I don't know how I would ever use it, but it's interesting!"

Darren: "Thanks! This is a state of the art potato masher. I know it may look intimidating, but it is in the incredible piece!"

Margaret: "A potato masher? I would have never guessed; it looks so high tech! What would you ever need such a fancy piece for? I've had the same one for years and it works just fine."

Darren: "Funny you should ask! What was your name again, friend?"

Margaret: "Margaret!"

Darren: "Well, Margaret, that is a beautiful name! This state of the art potato masher is an incredible piece that enables you to mash your potatoes into a creamy blend. You can also use it to rice your potatoes, which is a neat ability that I bet your potato masher can't do!"

Margaret: "No, it certainly can't!"

Darren: "One thing I love about this phenomenal potato masher is that it allows me to achieve a creamy texture that my old one couldn't. Plus, I don't have to put in any extra energy! It's easier! I get to enjoy extra potatoes *and* my arm doesn't hurt from mashing the entire pot!"

Margaret: "Oh! Yes, I certainly know what it is like to get a sore arm. You know, I find that to be troublesome, and I don't make potatoes often because of it. But still, it seems so much fancier! I don't even know how I would use it!"

Darren: "Here, Margaret, let me show you! See how it mashes this potato down so easily? My Mom loves this device because it makes the process so much easier. She says when we're having family dinner, she can still make my Dad's favorite rosemary and garlic mashed potatoes without having her arthritis act up in her wrist!"

Margaret: "Is that so? Wow!"

Darren: "Why don't you give it a try?"

Margaret: "Sure!"

Darren: "What do you think, Margaret?"

Margaret: "Well, it is certainly incredible! I can see myself using this. What would a piece like this cost me?"

Darren: "Margaret, it is your lucky day! This potato masher regularly costs $59.95, but today they went on sale for just $39.99!"

Margaret: "Oh my! $40 for a potato masher? That is a lot of money!"

Darren: "Well, Margaret, the thing about this incredible potato masher is that you are not only getting the masher, but the ricer. It also comes with this extremely soft grip handle to ensure that it is easy for absolutely anyone to use! That means when you replace your old one with it, you will be certain to keep this one for many years, too! Plus, it has a lifetime warranty!"

Margaret: "I'll take one!"

In the above scenario, Darren learned Margaret's name and used charm to help her feel comfortable with him. He also ensured that he regularly talked about how incredible the potato masher was. When Margaret expressed concerns that the potato masher was expensive, he used proof to explain why it was such an awesome piece and repeated the value she was getting in a few unique ways before allowing her to make the final decision. You can also see where deceit was used, as Darren did not discuss the price until after Margaret had already used the product and admitted she liked it.

These techniques worked naturally in the conversation and enabled Darren to take the lead. Margaret showed up at the supermarket that day with no intention of leaving with a new potato masher, and Darren began his pitch with Margaret with no intention of letting her leave without one. He did not push it on her or at any time or make her feel as though she was being pressured into the sale. Instead, he used repetition, proof, and emotions to help her see why she needed the potato masher so badly. This allowed him to make the sale in a way that did not in any way suggest that he was brainwashing Margaret into believing that she truly needed the potato masher.

Scenario two: going on a date

Getting someone to go on a date with you can sometimes be difficult. Many times, we pull back or even avoid asking anyone out, fearing rejection. Luckily, mind control techniques can be used not only to help you build your confidence but also to land you the date you want to go on.

The following scenario is one between Jason (the asker) and Louise (the one who wants to be asked.) See if you can identify the areas where mind control is used before we even begin discussing it at the end of the conversation.

Jason: "Hey, Louise! Long time no see. How is my old pal doing?"

Louise: "Hey, Jason, I'm good thanks. Just went out on an incredible date last night with this guy from work. We probably won't do it again, but I had a lot of fun anyway!"

Jason: "That sounds great! What did you guys do?"

Louise: "Well, he took me to laser tag, which seems very juvenile! I was hoping he would take me to dinner and show me his mature side, but he never did. Guys can be like that, you know?"

Jason: "I guess!"

Louise: "Well what did you do the last time you took a girl on a date, Jason?"

Jason: "We went out to eat at a local lobster restaurant! The drinks there was killer. Have you ever been?"

Louise: "I haven't! It sounds amazing. Maybe one day someone will treat me to date like that!"

Jason: "Maybe!"

Louise: "Speaking of lobster, it has been a long time since I've had any. I wonder who would want to go with me!"

Jason: "Why don't you and I go together? I'll treat you to the date you are looking for!"

Louise: "Oh! Sure!"

In this short conversation, Louise brings up the fact that she wants to go on a date, but is disappointed that men are always immature when she agrees to go. She has fun but doesn't see the relationship going anywhere because she wants someone more mature. Jason admits that he takes his dates to places such as the local lobster restaurant. Louise wants to go on a date with Jason and experience what it would be like to date someone who is mature and can hold a conversation through dinner. She continues to talk about dates and brings up the fact that she would love to go on one. When Jason talks about lobster, Louise paraphrases his conversation by speaking about lobster and how much she would enjoy a date like that. Jason then asks Louise out. Louise planted the idea of going on a date together all along but allowed Jason to feel as though he was the one responsible for coming up with the idea. She used deceit to make it seem as though she was planning on asking someone else to go when in reality she wanted Jason to ask her.

Scenario three: getting a promotion

Getting a promotion may seem difficult, but when you are a master at brainwashing, it can be extremely easy. In the following scenario, you will learn how Linda (the employee) brainwashes George (the boss) into giving her a promotion.

George: "Linda, do you know why I have called you into my office today?"

Linda: "It is my two-year review, right?"

George: "That's right, Linda! I want to talk about how you are doing in your job. Would you like to share your thoughts with me?"

Linda: "Well, George, I think I have been doing well! Recently Susanne got laid off, so I have had to pick up a lot of the slack with her being gone. I have been handling it well, though! Terri, our supervisor, seems to be unaware of how much of a struggle this can be. I often find everyone coming to me for help because he simply doesn't understand what needs to be done!"

George: "It sounds like you have been taking on a lot of extra responsibility lately. I have seen you taking part in a lot more activities at work lately, too, which I like."

Linda: "Yes! Well, you know I'm coming after your job, George! One day I'm going to run this show"

George: "Ha ha, I won't be leaving any time soon!"

Linda: "Well, good! I still have more to learn from you. I do wish I could have more responsibility, though. With everyone coming to me for help, I feel as though I could assist them more if I had more authority on the floor. If a position like Terri's ever opened up, I would like to be considered for it, please!"

George: "Well, Linda, I will keep that in mind! In the meantime, let's discuss your sales. How have your numbers been?"

Linda: "Oh they have been incredible! I have been feeling confident in my ability to help customers find what they are looking for and get the products that serve their needs. This truly is such an amazing job. I look forward to coming to work every day and am grateful to have found a company where I can stay for a long time! I also appreciate the opportunity to grow into more advanced positions over time!"

George: "That sounds amazing, Linda! I'm happy you are feeling so confident in your position. Look, I don't have any supervisory roles right now, but I do have a sales leadership position. What do you say we put you in that position and start training you to take over the next supervisor role that becomes available? It will come with the added responsibility you desire, and a raise to compensate you for the extra work you will be doing around here!"

Linda: "Wow, thank you so much, George! I appreciate it!"

You can see how easily Linda led this conversation the entire time. She always answered George's questions but was able to turn the answers around to repeat that she wanted to be promoted to a higher position within the company. She started by saying that she wanted to go for George's position as a manager but then scaled back to say that she only wanted to be put in a supervisor position. This ensured that George didn't feel threatened by her intentions and also proved that she wanted more within the business. She also used his name regularly, as we know this is a powerful method of seducing someone into feeling trusting and comfortable around you. Linda used proof to show that she was already doing incredibly well in her position and was shouldering many responsibilities above her current level. This proved she was capable of meeting the needs of the company. As a result, George wanted to compensate her for her hard work and ensure that she would remain faithful to the company, as she expressed that she already was. This is how you can easily use mind control to get a promotion at work!

The above situations are excellent real-life scenarios that show exactly how natural and effortless mind control strategies are once you have practiced them. In each conversation, the brainwasher was entirely in control and knew exactly what to say to get the other person to do what they wanted them to do. Everything was natural and comfortable, and nothing was forced.

The great strategy of repetition was used throughout every conversation, and you can see how it contributed to helping the listener adopt the opinion of the person leading the conversation. This is a powerful tool and should never be overlooked. This is essentially the way you can change someone's mind, without ever having to convince them to believe something new.

When you master the art of mind control, you will find that these scenarios are exactly what your natural abilities will represent. You will have very natural conversations that flow smoothly and yet still get you the exact results you desire. Everything else will come easily because you have mastered the art of brainwashing. Remember, it takes time, but it can be easy for you, too!

Chapter 6:
Manipulation Secrets

You must learn how to build trust with your target before you get them to behave the way that you want. No one is going to do what you ask if they don't know you, and they are even less likely to do what you want if they don't even trust you. While you are working on some of the other techniques in this guidebook, make sure you are building up as much trust as you can with the target.

Learn to understand how you are manipulated every single day and get rid of the chains of manipulation

There are a few different things you can do to build up the trust you want with your target. Some of these include:

Always be transparent. When you are trying to sell something to the target, whether a product or a specific course of action, never lie or misrepresent information about it. It is so easy for your target to talk to other people or go online, and it will not take them long to figure out that you have misled them. If the target asks you some questions, you need to answer as honestly as possible. If you happen not to know the answer, that is fine. Let the target know that you don't have the answer, but you will be happy to go and find it out.

Know how to communicate with your target audience. It is hard to build up trust with your target if you know nothing about them. You need to listen to both what they are saying and their body language to help you figure out what sets them off, what is important, and what you can do to impress them along the way.

The best way to do this is to spend time with your target. While you may think that you only need to talk to a target on occasion, or even once, it is really all about building up a relationship. You need to talk to them regularly, at least a few times before you can get them to feel their trust in you. The good news is that the more time you spend with the target, the easier it will be to understand them and use that information to your advantage.

Make and keep promises. Your target is going to be watching you so make sure you are consistent so they trust you. This means you need to give them something they can trust. Making and then keeping promises will make it easier for the customer to gain some trust in working with you. Some of the things you can do to help build up this trust through promises include:

- Offer to help them out with a project at work.
- Promise that you will meet them at a certain time for a meeting and show up on time, if not early.
- If they tell you a secret, keep that secret no matter what.

You will find that being consistent with what you do and say will make all the difference to the target. When your target comes to understand that they can trust you because of the way you act, they are more likely to take your advice and do what you "suggest" to them.

Be honest. While all the other techniques in this guidebook can be great ways to work on manipulating your target, the best and most authentic way is to be honest. When you are honest, there is nothing to hide from them. You don't need to worry about slipping up or making mistakes. A good manipulator is successful because he is honest with the target, rather than trying to hide information and facts. A lot of people out there assume they need to spend their time lying to manipulate their target. But the truth is, when you start lying , it is going to go against all of the things you are trying to do. Once your target finds out, and they are going to find this out at some point or another, they will keep their guard up every time they come near you, making it almost impossible to get them on your side ever again.

Remember that we talked about trust when it comes to manipulating your target. If trust is gone or broken, then it is almost impossible to manipulate that person again. This is particularly true if you are working in a professional environment. Honesty is the best policy, no matter how tempting it can be to tell a few lies to make your point sound better. Your target is going to appreciate the honesty you bring to the table, and you will get so much further when you remain honest with them all the time.

Confidence shows you know what you're talking about. Let's take a look at an example to see how this one can work for your needs. Let's say you walk into a mattress store and look around. You are greeted by a nice salesperson who is well dressed, looks you in the eye, and seems confident in their knowledge of the store and how they can help you. They walk you through some of the options while maintaining a smile and good composure.

On the other hand, you walk into the same mattress store and you are greeted by a salesman who seems quite nervous, who barely looks at you at all, much less looks you in the eyes. He barely knows what he is talking about and is sweating like a pig, indicating he would like to be anywhere rather than helping you out.

Out of the two scenarios above, in which would you be more willing to purchase a mattress? You would likely purchase a mattress from the first salesperson, even if you had just walked in to look around with no intention of purchasing a mattress. The same thing can be said when you are working with manipulation.

If you want the other person to pay attention to what you are saying, you need to show that you are confident in what you are saying. You need to show that you are interested in the other person, that you know what you are talking about, and that you are sure you are providing them with the best option for their needs.

For those not able to show confidence to their target, you are going to be disappointed in what you achieve. It is time to gain that confidence or learn how to fake it if you want any chance of manipulating another person to do what you would like.

Overcome everyday flattery, lying deception, and bribery

One of the worst things you can do when working on manipulating your target is to lie. You may think this is the best option because then you can say whatever you like to get the other person to believe you. You may think this is the only way to get the other person even interested. Most of the time, you assume they will never find out, and you will be able to keep on manipulating them without repercussions.

Unfortunately, no matter how good you are at lying, these lies are going to end up coming back to haunt you. The target will at some point find out that you have been lying, and when they do, that trust between the two of you will be gone. Once the trust is gone, you will never be able to manipulate that person again. Now, there are a few main reasons why a manipulator may try to lie to their target, and none of them are good signs. Some of the most common reasons include:

- They don't know what they are selling: if you are not an expert in the topic at hand, it can be hard to stick with one story. These individuals might add on facts or change things up because they want to still look knowledgeable; so they make things up, or they don't want to share the truth with the target because it makes them feel guilty.
- They are empathetic: some people will lie because they feel insecure about themselves as well as their relationship with the target. They want the target to like them no matter the cost, so they choose to stretch the truth a bit. But since this ends up breaking the bond of trust, it will backfire.
- You worry about the final result (such as money): if you are only interested in manipulating the other person to make money, you may be willing to lie to get the person to agree with what you are saying. This can be dangerous in the long run. The target will find out that you have been lying, and you will lose that result and the money that goes with it.

Even though you are trying to manipulate the other person to do what you want, it is still important to build up a good relationship along the way. And lying is one of the quickest ways to break that relationship and make the person want to have nothing to do with you. Stick with the truth, and you will get the best results with your target.

Consider using bribery

Another technique you can try is bribery. This is a pretty common one that people choose to use, and it can work like a charm if you do it right. The point here is that you need to reward the other person, whether it is materially or emotionally, so they feel they need to return the favor.

Now, you do need to do this properly and make it a bit subtler than just saying, "I'll hand you ten dollars if you do what I want." Most people are too smart for this to work. But there are still some ways that you can use bribery to help you out.

Of course, there are times when you and the other person will come together to meet the common goals of both parties. You and the other person may both need something, so you can use a form of bribery to get what you want. If you and the other person are aware of what is going on in this transaction, then there is nothing wrong with making sure the situation goes the way you would like.

However, there are usually a few steps that need to occur. You want to make sure you can get the other person indebted to you in some way. You need to do them some kind of favor or help them out, so they feel that they need to help you out at some later point.

If you have something that you want someone else to help you out with, then it is a good idea to start looking for opportunities to do them a favor. Once you do this, you are going to get the person indebted to you, and it will be much easier to manipulate them.

So, let's say you have a coworker who has an emergency with their family. They need to get a presentation or a big project started. You could jump in and offer to help, so they can go and deal with the family emergency. You may have to take on a little bit of extra work, but then the other person is going to feel indebted to you, and it will be much easier to convince the them to do what you want.

The sooner you can ask for your favor after you have helped the other person, the better the result will be. If the other person says, "Thank you for helping me out with x. Is there anything I can help you out with?" that is the perfect time to present your argument and ask them for something. They just offered to help you and may feel awkward if they back out at that point. This is the time when they are the most likely to agree with you, no matter what you are offering.

Decoding physical contact

When it comes to creating a good relationship with your target, you will find that using touch can help you out. It creates an intimate bond for a small moment. It can say a lot without you ever needing to say a word. The meaning of touch can be easily understood, which is harder to do with some gestures and words.

While all humans respond to touch, how can you use the power of touch to manipulate another person? Take note that you are not using touch to physically force someone to do what you want. It is meant to be a gentle approach, one that can help to build trust, which makes it the perfect tool for a manipulator. Studies show how touch can increase the likelihood that someone will do a favor for you if you ask. This is because touching shows trust and sincerity, and for some reason, it makes it harder for someone to disagree or say no to you.

This makes touching a good technique to use if you would like to ask your target to do some favor for you. But along with the touching, you need to add sincerity to the movement, or the other person will feel that the touch is kind of weird. And you need to use this technique as sparingly as possible. It is not going to work best if you talk to a random person and touch them multiple times during the same meeting.

Remember that with this strategy, you need to make the touch appropriate. If you are a man trying to use this strategy on a woman, make sure that you are touching her in a way that she would not think anything was wrong with it. This touch needs to show your good intentions, not make someone feel uncomfortable with you.

Of course, this is not always a guaranteed successful strategy. Some people do not like to be touched at all, and if you try to use this strategy on them, they will instantly get tense and refuse to listen to you. This is why it is so important to pay attention to your target and learn from their cues before you get started.

Touching is considered a strong language. It can be effective when asking for favors, so reserve it for when you want something from another person. Also, if you want to show the other person that you are on their side and sympathize with them, using touch can be a great option as well.

While you are talking to your target, you must work on the eye contact you have with them. This eye contact is going to help you create a deep connection with your target and can even create some intimacy between the two of you. If you find that making this eye contact is uncomfortable, it is time to get over it and move on. There are many tricks that will make using proper eye contact easier. You are never going to convince the other person to trust you if you are not able to look them in the eye.

There are a lot of benefits to using proper eye contact with your target. Eye contact shows that you are giving the target your full attention and you find them to be very important in your life. It is also a sign that you are being sincere in what you are saying. Also, it is a good way to read what the other person is thinking.

For example, if you are unsure of what the other person is thinking, or if they are trying to lie to you, you can ask them a series of questions while keeping eye contact. Then move on to some questions that are more sensitive. This is a good way to catch the target off guard. If you notice that the person looks away suddenly when answering your key questions, it means that they are feeling guilty or are uncomfortable with talking about it. Either way, it shows you something that you may not have realized otherwise about the person.

Keep in mind that while you are making eye contact, it does not give you an excuse to ignore some of the other gestures the target is making. It is your job to pay attention to as much as possible and be observant when it comes to talking to the other person. You can also practice looking away from the target on occasion so your eye contact does not getting too intense or extreme. Any time you want to stress one of your points to the target, it is best to do so while making direct eye contact, and always look directly at the person when you are actively listening.

Be more seductive

Manipulating a target comes when presenting them with an object of desire and withholding it until the target acts. The object may be the seducer or some other asset, like money. Scam emails from Nigerian princes work by seducing the target with the prospect of easy money.

Sexual seduction may include provoking irrational behavior, based on the promise of endorphins. An alternative way of viewing this is as persuasion to manipulate the goals of others, prioritizing a sexual encounter above everything else.

Seduction revolves around power, as it is presenting and persuading the ability to offer somebody what they want. Bonus points to you if you recognized that this is hardly distinct from the "carrot."

Use effective communication

An effective communication skill you can use is to repeat certain words and phrases when you are talking to another person. While the conscious mind is known to have a more limited focus, your subconscious can focus on everything going on around you. Also, this subconscious is not going to forget what is taking place. This means that whatever message you try to imprint into the subconscious is not going to be forgotten and can have a big influence on the decision-making process for your target.

Let's say that you would like to convince your spouse that it is time to get things more sensual in the bedroom that night. You probably do not want to just get home and jump into bed. Your partner might not be in the mood because they were not expecting it at all. However, you can use certain keywords, ones connected to being sensual, and start to pepper them into the conversation you are having with your spouse that night.

The words do not have to just be about sex. They can be things like bed, scent, wet, flowers, and so on. You can pick just a few of these, usually one to three keywords, and then repeat them over and over again as you talk to your spouse.

You will need to repeat these keywords at least a few times during the conversation, but the more, the better. Since you are working with the subconscious mind, it is going to take a little bit of time for the target to respond the way you would like. The message is getting there, and it will not be forgotten, but you have to be patient and keep using those words, more than once, throughout the night.

You do need to take some precautions when using this strategy. You do not want to let the other person know that you want to imprint messages on their subconscious mind, or they will stop listening to you. This takes away trust, and we already know that once the confidence and trust are gone, you will not be able to manipulate them any longer.

So, how often are you going to need to repeat those keywords to get them to stick? There isn't a rule as to how often you will need to repeat the keywords. The idea is to repeat these words as many times as you can in the conversation while making it all sound natural. So, do not say the words a hundred times every ten minutes, but if you can add them in naturally, then go ahead and do it.

There are times when you will not need to repeat the keywords, although this is not normal. There are going to be times when your target is going to respond to the keywords on a conscious level right after you say them. This will happen if that keyword was already established and simply by hearing the word, it will have the intended effect.

One last thing to remember about keywords is that they need to be relevant to the conversation at hand. If you want the target to respond in a certain way, you need to use keywords that will prime them to act as such. If you wanted the target to get more sensual in the bedroom, for example, then it would make no sense to bring up keywords about food or going on a vacation.

While we spent time talking about how we need to stop and use silence to our advantage when manipulating a target, you must learn to listen as well. It is never a good idea to spend all the time talking to the target and never listening to what they are saying. When you listen, you learn a lot more than when you are talking the whole time. Listening is a hard habit for a lot of people to acquire, but once you can do this, it is much easier to learn about your target and use that information to your advantage.

There are a lot of different ways to listen better to your targets.

Pay attention

You need to make sure that you are giving all your attention to the target while they are talking. You also need to acknowledge the message they are sending to you. Pay attention to non-verbal communication in this process as well because that can speak louder than words. Some of the ways you can pay attention to your target include:

- Listen to their body language
- Do not become distracted by side conversations or other environmental factors
- Do not prepare for a rebuttal right away
- Get rid of the distracting thoughts in your head
- Look directly at the speaker

Find ways to show that you are listening. You need to learn how to use gestures and body language to show the target that you are paying full attention to them. Some of the ways that you can do this include:

- Encourage the target to keep on speaking by using small verbal comments, such as, "Yes," "Uh huh," and "I agree."
- Smile and use your facial expressions to react to some of the things the target is saying.
- Nod on occasion.
- Take care to notice your posture and ensure that it is inviting and open all at once.

Provide feedback. As the expert, there are times when you will need to provide feedback to your target. The only way you can do this effectively is if you are listening. Some ways include:

- Summarize what you are hearing to ensure that you understand it.
- Ask questions to help you clarify some points.
- Redirect what has been said. Paraphrasing can help with this.

Defer judgment. It is a big waste of time to interrupt the other person, and it can leave both of you frustrated in the end. It can even limit a full understanding of the message being shared. Ways you can defer judgment include:

- Do not interrupt the target with a counter-argument
- Allow the speaker a chance to finish their points before you start asking questions

Respond in the appropriate manner. Active listening is a good way to show that you respect the target and understand what they are saying. You are doing this to gain a new perspective and information on the target. Some of the ways you can respond appropriately to your target include:

- Treat the other person in the way you would like to be treated, or at least that you think they would want to be treated

- When you add in your opinions, make sure you respectfully do this
- Be honest, candid, and open with the responses that you give, without being cruel

Control your emotions

Another thing to work on is mastering your emotions. If you want to manipulate another person, you need to be in total control. As soon as you let your emotions get out of hand, you have lost the game and will find it almost impossible to gain control back over the target.
A good manipulator is someone who can master their emotions well. When someone argues with them or says something they do not like, they can talk through it or shrug it off. You want to play on the emotions of your target, but if you are emotional, it is more likely that you will become the one who is manipulated.
So, how do you learn how to better master your emotions and get the control that you would like in life? Some of the options include:

- Wake up each morning and choose some positive emotions. Think about optimism, love, and happiness from the moment you get up. This helps you to get into a good mood right away.
- There will be times when you are going to feel negative emotions. It is fine to embrace these emotions like anger, disappointment, fear, frustration, and hurt. When they come up, feel them rather than ignore them, and try to figure out how you can make things better.
- Do not bury things deep inside. While it is not a good idea to burst out in anger when talking to your target, it is wise to own your emotions. Recognize that they are there and legitimate, and deal with them right away rather than hide them.
- Move around. Sometimes emotions of sadness and anger can be cured by being active. Try to do some exercise each day or go for a walk any time you are feeling down.

- Develop new habits each day. Sometimes we are dealing with negative emotions because we feel we are not accomplishing anything. If you learn new habits or take up a new hobby upon occasion, you will find that it is easier to master these emotions.
- Write out a list of ten things that are good in your life. It can be anything you like, as long as it helps you to focus on these good things and feel better.

You must be able to control your emotions as much as possible. Manipulating your target is not always going to go the way you want. But if you explode at the target or are not able to control yourself as you are supposed to, your goals are going to become visible, and you will not see success.

Chapter 7:
Psychology Facts About Manipulation

Some people are naturals at reading others, but they couldn't tell you how they know what they know. That's because they are intuitively reading others' body language, but they don't have the knowledge to define why they are such good communicators. More than 70 percent of the messages we send and receive are through non-verbal language. Not only are the greatest percent of our messages non-verbal, but that non-verbal language is more honest and genuine than the words we speak. Our bodies don't sugarcoat the message; we just respond and react without being conscious of doing so.

If people are saying one thing but their body language is delivering a different message, put more stock in what you see than what you hear. However, to make sure you are reading the person correctly, let's discuss all the different nonverbal messages we send. We'll cover nonverbal signals and what they might mean, but keep in mind that different cultures and countries might attach a different meaning to body language. When you're confused about the non-verbal message that another is sending, then listen to the words and take the signals in context with the phrases they use.

Another way to determine the message is through the tone, pitch, and volume of another's voice. It gives truth to that saying, "It's not what you said but how you said it." When all these things are examined during your analysis of others, you'll find clarity in the message. While we're at it, there is one more thing—pay attention to the other person's required personal space. If you are questioning whether the message they are sending is positive, negative, or benevolent, step inside their personal space and be aware of their reaction. Their feelings will then be quite pronounced. If the message was meant to be off-putting, they will immediately step back or adopt a space-claiming stance that will let you know their feelings in no uncertain terms.

Facial expressions, features, and the head: playing with hair and moving the head. If someone slides their fingers through their hair at the temples and tosses their head back, this is an indication that they might be flirting. On the other hand, if they are running their fingers through their hair from their forehead through the top of their crown, that is a sign they are confused or frustrated. Tilting the head and twirling the hair is also a flirtatious mannerism, indicating interest combined with a little nervous tension.

When people nod their heads, it matters how many times they do so before stopping. For example, public speakers who are attentive to their audiences know that three nods mean interest and attentiveness. However, if you observe a group of people conversing, you'll notice the person who nods their head only once is eager to leave and will probably be the next one to make a quick exit.

If someone is interested in what you're saying, they will often tilt their head in your direction. They could be showing curiosity or questioning what you are saying when they bring one ear closer to make sure they are getting every detail of the conversation.

Eye movement. People usually blink six or seven times a minute, but those who are stressed blink quite a bit more. If someone covers their eyes with their hands, excessively rubs their eyes or closes their eyes, they could be hiding something or feel threatened. When the eyes are shifty or rapidly moving from one person to another, it reflects scattered thoughts are going on in their heads. If there is a flickering interest between two people when this is happening, it can also be a way for people to prevent detection as they checking out the other.

If someone has a habit of not making eye contact or looking down as they speak, it can show shyness or be a cry for empathy. They are waiting for you to ask what's wrong and open the way for them to share their feelings. Investigators have come to realize that a sustained glance from a person who denies involvement in a crime may mean they are lying and trying to over-compensate by looking them straight in the eyes for a long time to show they're telling the truth.

If you have posted a question and the person you asked looks upward, they are most likely trying to picture something. On the other hand, if they look to the side toward their ear, they could be trying to recall a message they heard. If they look downward after your question, they are connecting your question with something negative and trying to find a way to avoid answering or revealing their feelings about the matter.

Eyebrow movement. If an individual raises their eyebrows, it usually means the person is curious about or interested in your conversation. A quick popup of one eyebrow could be flirtation, and if the eyebrow is raised a bit longer, it often means that the other person doesn't quite buy into what you are saying. If the brows furrow, you can almost bet that person is having second thoughts about what is being done or said. It most likely indicates a negative emotion like fear or confusion, so it might be time for you to back off a bit.

Lips. Of course, a smile sends a universal message if it is truly a smile. We've all been at the other end of a fake smile, which is one that doesn't travel to the eyes and make them wrinkle in agreement. We call those "Red Carpet" smiles. They are Hollywood smiles given by people trying to be friendly to their fans but just want to get inside, sit down, and make it through the night.

Individuals who plaster a smile on their face almost all the time are usually nervous. If it's in the workplace, they could feel out-of-their-depth or incompetent. There's a good chance that foreigners who smile a lot don't understand a blasted thing, so they just smile and nod.

Another thing people do with their lips is suck on and bite them. Sucking or biting the lip is a reaction by those who need to settle themselves down. Like a newborn, the action soothes them and offers a bit of comfort in a stressful situation. If one clamps down on their lips or purses them, it can mean frustration or anger.

Body and limb movements and positions. If there is a group of people standing and talking and one or more opens their body to you, that is an invitation to join the conversation. If they just turn their heads, you might want to choose another group. You will know if you have captured the attention of a love interest because he or she will turn slightly toward you and point their feet in your direction, to indicate they are interested in finding out what makes you tick. If you step into the group and the person beside you touches your shoulder or arm, this is a direct ploy to show they are interested in exploring the relationship a bit further.

When you step into the group, if the person beside you leans, they genuinely like you. If their head retracts backward, perhaps something you said surprised or offended them. If they physically lean away, they've already made up their mind that they're not going to listen to or like you. If they turn their head in the opposite direction and follow it with their shoulder, you just got the cold shoulder. So, forget about it!

Standing positions. If someone is standing with legs about shoulder-width apart, it often is a sign of dominance and determination, as if they needed to stand their ground against something or prove a point. If they stand with legs together, front forward, they will hear you out, but you need to make your point quickly. When the person you are speaking with is standing and shifting their weight from side to side or front to back, it could indicate several things. They could be bored or anxious and need to soothe themselves with a rocking sort of movement. To determine their feelings, it is necessary to look further at what they are doing with their arms as well.

Arm positions. Don't assume that crossed arms always mean that the other person is upset. Not so! Some people will stand or sit with their arms crossed because it is just a comfortable position. You can distinguish the other's emotions by looking further at their facial expression. If they have furrowed eyebrows, a pursed mouth, and their arms are crossed, chances are they are angry or upset about something. Crossed arms can also be a sign of protection or a closed attitude to the ideas you are presenting.

If someone is talking with their arms flopping around, it can mean they are excited and agreeable, or it can say they are out of control. Again, you'll need to couple your observations with other nonverbal messages to be sure. Typically, people who are overly animated are less believable and have less control over their emotions, as well as a lack of power. They flail their arms to gain attention as if to say, "I'm talking now, so would somebody please listen to me?"

Leg and foot positions. People whose toes turn inward could be closing themselves off to your comments, or they could just be pigeon-toed. To determine if there is a physiological issue that causes their toes to point in, you might need more background information. Don't rush to judgment, just wait, observe more body language, and listen to their words. Some people who began turning in their toes because they were insecure or awkward might have created a habit they now find difficult to break. The only message they are sending is one that says, I have a physical issue that is impacting my body language.

Sitting positions. If a person is spread out all over your couch, they have a feeling of self-importance. On the other hand, they probably have a good deal of confidence as well. Legs open, leaning forward with elbows on knees shows an in-charge attitude that is still open to hearing what you have to say.

If a person is sitting next to you and crosses their legs at the knee, pointing their foot toward you, they are permitting you to approach them. If, however, they are sitting next to you and angle their body in the opposite direction, you're probably not going to engage or connect with him or her. If that same person is fidgeting, quickly moving their ankle or foot, they are looking for a way out. Excuse yourself; both of you will probably feel more comfortable.

Hands. When people sit on their hands, and the temperature isn't below freezing, it could be an indication that they are deceitful— trying to hide something from you. If they walk with their hands in their pockets or behind their back, they might be relaying information, but you're not getting the full picture because they are withholding it. When you look at one's fingers and see bitten nails or chewed cuticles, you can bet that this is a nervous person with low self-esteem. Or else they have put themselves in a situation they find extremely uncomfortable.

When someone holds their hands like a church steeple and presses them to their lips, they have something important to add to the conversation but are trying to decide how to present the information. They are self-assured and will contribute when the time is right. These are thinkers, analytical types.

If the person is rubbing their legs with open palms pressed down, they are feeling vulnerable or uncomfortable with your nearness or your conversation. If nothing is said, don't think you are not sending a message that is perhaps louder than any words. Examine your body language and see what message you are sending that could be creating this reaction.

Walking. People who advance with rather large strides are purposeful and therefore perceived as important and competent. People think those who walk with a little bounce in their step most likely have a positive nature. And those who walk hunched over with shoulders down—well, that kind of speaks for itself, doesn't it? They are probably prone to depression and wrapped a bit too tight.

What does their voice say about them? There are four indicators of the quality of one's voice. They are intonation, volume, pitch, and rate of speech. If the voice is monotone and rather flat, they are probably bored or boring. The lack of animation in the voice could also indicate the speaker is tired. If the person's voice sounds clear and concise, they most usually are confident and powerful, more like the Leader Personality Type. If the volume is quiet or soft, the person is thought to be shy, or it could even mean they have a secret they don't want to share.

Rate of speech is also quite important when analyzing others, especially if you are attempting to mirror them to increase the chance of connectivity. For example, Leader Personality Types will usually speak fast and loud, and you need to match their volume and rate. Identifiers often speak slower than Leaders, and their pitch is more soothing than the dominant personality type. The voice can be a strong descriptive element of the individual's personality type.

By now, you have probably caught on that every movement has a message. You know you can verify the meaning of some nonverbal language by other things, such as one's words, voice, facial expressions, and gestures. To discover the real message, you must become a student of human behavior, studying the other's movements, speech patterns, attitude, words, gestures, and expressions to analyze people successfully.

You've been introduced to nonverbal language and the four main personality types, and how you form accurate perceptions, but all these things are not separate from one another. They all blend to create effective communication.

Chapter 8:
How to Deal with a Manipulator and Avoid Manipulators

Cutting off manipulation ties

This chapter is the climax of the book. You might be reading this chapter mainly because you have had enough of being manipulated or living with manipulative friends, family members, or your significant others. You might have reached the "never again" point in your life after bad experiences with manipulation. Getting long-lasting solutions to manipulation could end life's challenges and make the world a better place to live. Not every manipulative act leads to success; some lead to distress. Before solving any manipulative deeds, you need to ask yourself the following:

After being manipulated, do you feel you have been taken advantage of?
Do you attempt to manipulate others?
What are the reasons if you have ever felt like manipulating others?
Do you regret failing to be smarter once you have been manipulated?
Can someone make you do what you do not want to do?
Do you feel guilty if you fail to do what people request you to do?
Do you feel angry, frustrated, or uncomfortable around specific people?

This is not the best time to ask why manipulators manipulate others, but it is the best time to know that they will never do it again to you.
Consider a case where you desperately need attention from your friends mainly because your parents did not give enough to you during your childhood. This attention could be sought from others because maybe your partner gives you none. In this case, you will have allowed people to manipulate you. You might fall for the "appraisal quotes": being told how beautiful or handsome you are or how amazing and different you are. Then you get manipulated in this kind of a fix. You will feel special and appreciated more than another person would. If you are a victim of this, you must have reached your final straw, and now you need solutions.

You should avoid being desperate. This means that after every bad experience, you should never go seeking attention immediately. Avoid contact with the manipulative person, especially after being hurt as they may end up taking advantage and keep manipulating you.

When a deal sounds and appears too good toa be true, you should not give in immediately. This can be helpful, especially in resisting some marketing manipulation tactics where salespersons try to persuade you to purchase a certain product is praised for its goodness and how amazing it is. You should buy what you want without being convinced to buy what you do not want or need.

Learn to control yourself even amid flattery. Note that too much flattery can mean manipulation is underway. Whenever people flirt too much or insist on getting a certain demand granted, always stop them immediately. Even if cooperation is good so far, it is bad at the same time as it can rub away your sound way of thinking.

You need to separate the "truly needful people" in your life from those "claiming to be in need". Some people genuinely need your help and you feel it is your responsibility or duty to help them. This may include your child, an aging parent, or a sick person. But some want to make you feel that their problem is your problem and their responsibilities are your responsibilities and you are supposed to deal with them. To sort out a manipulator from a truly needful person, ask a friend or relative who is objective and cool. If they say, "No," then that should be your response, too.

Manipulators may opt to get emotional to secure what they want, as described in the section on manipulative techniques or ways on to identify a manipulator. You should also learn how to deal with emotional manipulation. It is of no use trying to be straightforward with an emotional manipulator. This is because every statement you make is always turned down. Consider the case below:

You: I am so disappointed, you forgot my birthday!

Your friend: It makes me feel bad that you think I would by any chance forget your birthday. I wish I told you of the stress I have right now, but I did not want to stress you, too. I guess I should have valued your birthday, I am sorry.

82

In this case, your friend will even shed tears when responding. You will find yourself with nothing more to say and ending up babysitting your friend's angst. The solution to this is to trust your gut, senses, and instincts, and do not accept any apology or excuse that feels like nonsense.

An emotional persuader or manipulator always comes into the picture of a willing helper. Emotional manipulators will agree to what you ask them to do for you. When you say, "Thank you," they reply with sighs and non-verbal cues that insinuate that they do not want to really help you. When you question them, they will respond angrily and say you are unreasonable. The solution to this is to avoid challenging their sighs and make them accountable for their offer to help. Walk away to avoid crazy dramas.

Do not entertain them

In your relationships, you should never question your sanity. A manipulator will turn things around and justify that they never gave any promises. These manipulators lie a lot which can make you even doubt your senses. Carry a notebook and start making notes after every conversation, claiming that you feel you are so forgetful and they should not be worried about lapses. This helps you remove yourself from their range of intention and avoid manipulation.

To decrease your guilty feelings, be in-the-know that you are getting manipulated. Manipulators make you feel guilty for almost everything: too much caring, loving, emotions, nurturing, or support. Once you do anything for them, they never appreciate it and will even tell you that they did not expect whatever you did for them. You need to stop fighting other people's battles. Have a line to say to those manipulators who make you feel guilty. Tell them, "I have great confidence to be able do this. You are on your own." Sit back and listen to their response; they probably lack one.

You should avoid people who cannot talk to you or deal with issues directly. They always let you know everything through their friends, tending to send people to tell you what they want. Never entertain any connections they send you.

When manipulators are angry, they influence the environment and want everyone else to feel like them. They want to make people do things their way, by getting angry with everyone and expecting a friendly response. Remember, you also have your psychological issues and needs, so do not give in to such nonsense.

Anyone who is not accountable for their mess, taking no responsibility, and always complains about what other people do to them, is the kind of manipulator you should avoid at all costs. Never apologize for a mess that you are not responsible for. Leave the manipulator to realize their own mistakes. Avoid contact with these would-be manipulators. If you must, listen to them, but act differently. They cannot force you to get manipulated.

Setting personal boundaries can also be a long-lasting solution to manipulation. Before your relationship goes too far, and before anyone learns you inside out, set limits. You can state the kinds of behaviors you like or dislike. For instance, tell them they should not call you any time they feel like it past nine pm. Clearly define your goals so it will be possible to know when you are being manipulated. When you know your direction, it would be complicated for someone to influence you.

How to avoid manipulators

As you have read, it is easy to become part of someone's manipulations. You don't have to give into them, though. There are many ways to stop the cycle of emotional abuse and manipulation. We need to know how manipulators work to be able to avoid them altogether.

Manipulators are looking for something from you that they may not be getting from their own life or from themselves. Many are not happy with their lives, and they have very low self-esteem. They want to create problems for others to make themselves feel better. They love the idea of someone else feeling the pain they are feeling. If they can inflict this pain on others, they no longer worry about their feelings.

Some manipulators love the feeling of having power in any situation. They will find those they consider weak and persuade them to do what they want. The victims in these situations are generally bullied and will feel as if they have been dominated into doing things they never thought they would. In general, manipulators aren't all that bad. Some want very small things, while others will take anything that they can. Psychologists find them to be misguided and inconsiderate. So what are the best ways to stay away from manipulators? We have quite a few that can help you out.

Staying away from manipulators

Think about it: the easiest way to avoid being manipulated is just by staying away. Why does this seem to be so complicated, though? There are plenty of reasons why we allow ourselves to stay close to those who manipulate us. Manipulators, after all, learn how to control us in many ways. Most psychologists think it is learned behavior on their part. They have probably been a victim of it themselves, and it could have started as early as their childhood.

So if you cannot stay away from someone who is manipulating you, be very firm in your communication. Many of them will ask you questions over and over again until they get the answer they want. When you say yes to them, it means yes, but sometimes saying no could also mean yes. By being firm and saying the answer more than once, they should get the full picture. If they do continue to think you are saying yes, it could be time to get away from them and not think twice about it.

Ever hear that everyone has an inner child? Well, manipulators have an inner child, but it does not play and joke around as yours might. Most of the time, manipulators will only listen to that inner child to make decisions. If that inner child is telling them what to get out of people, they will turn into a manipulator to get what they want.

Manipulators have goals in mind when they push you to do something. Generally, these goals are to make you feel as if you are always doing something wrong. They also want to see just what they can get you to do for them. This is when firm words can help out. If they are not getting the point of your words across, use actions and body language to show that you are tired of them using and manipulating you.

It may surprise you, but manipulators can change, but they have to unlearn the behaviors they have been using on people. This can take quite a long time, but it is possible. Yes, they may be able to change, but if you cannot take the emotional abuse anymore, now is the time to get out. Perhaps you can give them a second chance when you have seen real change, but that is up to you.

This brings us back to why people can't leave abusive relationships. It is very easy for those of us who see the manipulation to tell our peers to leave the relationship. It isn't always the easiest thing to do, however. For one, our society has some strange ways of accepting unhealthy behavior and manipulations. The victim may not even be aware that anything is wrong in the relationship. If the victim has always been in these types of relationships, they may think it is the normal way that relationships work. If they think this is normal, they may look at you like you're crazy when you even suggest they leave.

Manipulation and emotional abuse are pretty crippling when it comes to our self-esteem. If you are being manipulated and want to leave, you may feel like you can't because you think that you will never find anyone else. If the victim is always feeling worthless, and they want to get out of the relationship, it can be quite difficult. They think of where they will go and who can they stay with. But sometimes, it is nearly impossible for them to get out of the relationship.

If the manipulation has gotten to the point of physical abuse, it may be very dangerous for the victim to feel they can leave. Chances are the manipulator is threatening them, and they could be afraid they will hurt them even more if they do leave. Many victims have been killed after leaving physically abusive relationships, and this is terrifying for those who are still in these relationships.

Lastly, our society makes it sound like no matter what we feel, we must stay with our partner forever. We must ride it out and think it will all get better. We do know that some manipulators can change, but not all of them will. It is up to the victim to get away from before it becomes too late.

Avoiding the manipulators

It is easy to say, avoid these predators, but it is not that easy to actually do. First, you need to see that they are manipulating you. Once you have decided this, you have to be careful about what you do. To acknowledge them, you will have to keep in mind that most of them do have specific traits. They know exactly how to find your weaknesses. When they figure out what your weakness is, they will use it to their advantage and against you. They will try to get you to give up the things you love. For example, many predators and manipulators will try to get your family to turn against you. There will be no shoulder to cry on when they don't want to see you or talk to you anymore. They will also try to get you to give up your hobbies and other things you love.

You do not have to put up with any of this. You can choose to ignore them and hope they will go away and stop trying to get at you. Once you have noticed they are trying to manipulate you, say no to them. You don't have to do everything they ask of you. This is where many people have trouble. They want to be kind and polite and not hurt anyone's feelings. You can say no to people. If they are trying to manipulate you, they will more than likely become furious when you tell them no, but this will give you a sure sign that they are trying to manipulate you.

When you have discovered that they are manipulating you, keep your distance. In different situations, you may notice the manipulator acting a lot differently. This is a sure-fire way to know that they are trying to manipulate you. Sometimes, they may act politely to you but so rude to anyone who tries to befriend you. Once you notice this, give them the space they need. You will see how they react, which will help you determine just how much they are trying to manipulate you.

It is important that if you do fall victim to a manipulator, please do not blame yourself. They know what they are doing when they choose you to be the one to manipulate. They know your weaknesses and want you to blame yourself. You will be able to figure out if they are manipulating you by seeking the answer to the question of being treated with respect? If you answer no immediately, you are the victim, and it is time to get out of the situation.

It will throw them off when you start turning the tables on them. Ask them questions that will make them think you know what they are doing to you. Find out why they think their demands are reasonable and how this situation will benefit you. When you turn the tables on them, they may do the running away. Always trust your judgment when it comes to asking questions. They may be a very good liar, so ask a few questions that will get them to think about what they are doing to you.

Many victims of manipulators have to reinvent themselves not to let it happen to them again. How do you do this? Part of reinventing yourself is to learn how to say no when these manipulators start to ask you to do things for them. They have already seen your vulnerable side, and now they want to attack it. If you put up emotional walls and make it so they cannot see your vulnerability, you will be able to stop them in their tracks! You also need to stop compromising when they want you to do something. Just keep telling them that you don't want to. Eventually, they should get the point, but if they don't, it is time to walk away.

Respecting yourself is another way to make sure they stop manipulating you. Once again, they will see this when you are confident and self-aware. They may even feel threatened by your new sense of self. This will act in your favor when they finally decide to call it quits with their manipulation.

Chapter 9:
Tips and Tricks to Defend Yourself from Manipulation

Now that we have gone over some of the methods and tactics people use to negatively manipulate others, it's time to talk about how to avoid these very methods. Negative manipulation can be defined as convincing others to do whatever you desire, without offering something of value back.

How does this phenomenon work?

A threat and no value. If a person says, "Help me finish this project or I'm going to be angry with you," they are trying to negatively manipulate your actions. They are not offering anything of value in return. However, if a friend offers you something of value in return for a favor, that isn't negative manipulation at all, because you're getting something back for the effort you put in.

Making another responsible for their emotions. Another form of manipulation is telling someone they are responsible for how you feel and they should feel guilty for it. For example, telling them if they don't come to your party, you will be highly disappointed. This implies it's their fault how you feel. However, if you offer to introduce your friend to someone they have been wanting to meet at your party, you are offering a situation that allows both of you to win.

Different types of negative manipulation

Turning your emotions against you. Techniques for manipulation vary widely, but usually, negative manipulators will attempt to get others' feelings to work against them. They will try to do this by doing or saying things intended to stir up fear, anger, shame, guilt, or any other uncomfortable feeling. For example, they might insinuate that if you don't follow through on their suggestions or orders, something horrible will result.

Threats of future unpleasantness. They might also try to describe all of the different types of unpleasant situations that could arise if you don't do what they want. They might imply or even overtly insist that something is your fault, responsibility, or duty, using ethics and morality to pressure you to come around to their ideas or demands. Some people will even throw every trick at you, warning you of the consequences of disappointing or letting them down.

Common phrases. They might imply that they will be so happy if we do what they want us to do and they will love us so much. They may use phrases like, "You need to..." or "You must..." or "You should..." as a way to subtly pressure you into following through on what they are asking of you. They will say those phrases and others that insinuate great consequences if you don't follow the obligation they are presenting.

What do each of the above methods and techniques share in common? The person doing the negative manipulation doesn't offer anything of value in return for fulfilling their wishes. Instead, the victim gets exploited by a created power imbalance.

How to avoid being negatively manipulated by others

Be aware of your rights. The absolute most important rule you can follow when dealing with someone who wants to manipulate you in a negative way is to know your worth and rights. This way, you will always know when someone is attempting to violate them. So long as others are not harmed in the process, you should defend yourself. Every human has the right to have differing opinions from others, to protect themselves and say "no" when they need to, and to decide what's important. You should have the right to express your wants, opinions, and feelings, and always be treated with respect.

Unfortunately, the world is full of people who won't want to acknowledge or respect your rights, especially the negative manipulators. You will come into contact with others who generally wish to take advantage of any opportunity. However, you can proudly defy this by letting them know that you are the one who runs your life, and no one else.

Maintain a healthy distance. Another way to tell who is manipulative is to pay attention to the way they act in varying situations and in front of various individuals. Although everyone, to a degree, puts on different faces depending on where they are, most people who are harmfully manipulative are extreme about it. They might, for example, be extremely polite and friendly to one person and completely disrespect another. They may act like a victim one second and then act in a controlling manner immediately after.

If you notice someone acting this way regularly, it's a good to distance yourself and not engage with them unless it's an absolute necessity. Usually, the reasons behind this type of behavior are complicated, and it isn't your duty or responsibility to help or change that person. Trying to do so will often only lead to suffering on your part, so it's better not to expect much when you notice these signs.

Don't blame yourself. A person who wishes to manipulate others in harmful ways searches for weaknesses to exploit, so it makes sense that someone who has been victimized by one might blame themselves or feel inadequate. But in a situation like this, you should remember that it isn't you who is the issue here; you are being pressured to feel bad by someone else who is very good at making people feel bad.

This is how they get their way. Instead, think about the relationship you have with this person and ask yourself if they are respecting you, demanding reasonable things of you, and whether you are both benefiting, or only one of you is. Also ask yourself if you feel good about yourself after spending time with this person, or if you would feel better being around them less. The way you answer these questions will lead to important answers about where the issue lies in the situation.

Question them. Eventually, this type of person is going to demand or request things from you. Many times, these requests or others will consider their needs, while more often completely ignoring yours. Next time you receive a solicitation that is completely unreasonable, turn the focus back to them by asking some questions. Ask them if their request is reasonable, or if what they are asking from you is fair. You can also try asking if you get to have an opinion in this matter or what benefit you will be gaining from the arrangement.

Each time you ask questions like this, you are holding a mirror up to them, allowing them to see what they are truly asking of you. If they are self-aware, they will likely retract their request or demand. But there may be some cases, such as when dealing with a narcissist, when the person will keep insisting without even considering your questions. If that happens, follow these guidelines.

Don't answer immediately. One way to combat manipulation is to use time as a resource. Often, the manipulator will not only ask you to fulfill an unreasonable demand, but they will want an answer immediately. When this happens, rather than answering right away, use time and distance yourself from their request and influence. This can be done by telling them that you will think about it. Although these words are simple, they give power back to you, giving you the option to weigh the advantages and disadvantages of the situation and let you work out something better, if need be.

Teach yourself to say "no". Saying "no" is difficult for many people, since we are often taught and conditioned to be polite whenever possible. Being able to say "no" confidently but politely comes with communication skills. When this is articulated effectively, you can hold onto your self-respect and also continue a healthy relationship. Keep in mind that your rights include deciding what matters to you, being able to turn down a request free from guilt, and choosing health and happiness for yourself. You are responsible for your life, not that of the person who is making unreasonable demands of you.

Create a consequence. Next time a negative manipulator tries to violate your rights and refuses to accept your answer, set a consequence for their behavior. Knowing how to assert and identify appropriate consequences is a crucial skill for standing down to someone who is being very difficult or disrespectful. If you can articulate this clearly and thoroughly, your consequences will cause them to pause and stop violating you, making them shift to a position of respect.

How to confront a bully safely. Not all manipulators resort to bullying, but many do. Someone is a bully when they use intimidation or harm to get what they want from you. Remember, always, that a bully chooses people they see as weak to pick on, and your compliance and passivity will only strengthen this. However, a lot of bullies are afraid and insecure deep down, so when the victim starts to stand up for himself, this will often lead the bully to back off. Whether this situation occurs on a playground or at the office, it applies most of the time. Keep in mind that many bullies have withstood bullying and violence. Although this doesn't excuse their behaviors, it does help the victim to understand.

Your influence skill set
Clarity of purpose

An important facet of the ability to influence others is clarity. Know what you want and have a clear plan of how you're going to get it. Whether you're working in sales, trying to improve the team's quarterly figures, or encouraging a student to be more diligent or start on the right career path, know what the objective is. The only way you can succeed in influencing someone to behave in a desired way is if you are clear about what you hope to achieve. You don't get in your car to drive to a destination you've never been to before without setting the GPS. The same goes for the application of influence toward achieving a desired effect or goal. Know where you're going.

Always be prepared in advance with the following:

- A list of prioritized objectives
- A clear picture of the final destination (what it looks like)

Preparing the environment

If you are seeking to reach an agreement with someone, you need to make them feel comfortable. You also need to be relaxed yourself. At the same time, for effective communication (which is important when you want to influence someone's behavior), you need to make the environment conducive to your interaction. You need to have in place a planned sequence of events beforehand.

The best way to achieve this is to draw up a meeting agenda and circulate it to those who will attend, at least one day before the meeting. In this way, everyone knows what to expect and what shape the meeting will take. The agenda should make clear what the goals of the meeting are. Checking off the items on it should move you closer to agreement, if not enable all present to reach a consensus to move forward. The logical sequence of events represented by following an agenda is a function of a critically structured plan. Having a plan of such quality never fails to impress.

Consensus building

In building a consensus, you are making it clear that you are open to suggestions (which you should always be, regardless of your single-minded focus on your ultimate goal). Hearing what people say and truly listening means you're not planning a response while they're talking. It means you're actively hearing everything they say. Subtext, word choice, and tone are all important and so are your skills at discerning what's being said. Proceeding with these skills can provide you with the basis for a genuine and not false consensus.

A false consensus is reached when people are "heard out", but not "heard". These are two entirely different animals. The first is the condescending indulgence of hearing what no longer matters because a decision has already been made and the results of that decision have been imposed. Being heard means that your influence on the final decision is still a possibility and what's offered might result in concessions if it features actual merit.

Being open to the input of others and being able to integrate their thoughts and suggestions into an existing plan is a function of leadership. Leadership is not imposed: it is extended to others as a service. Consensus building is a way to bring forward the knowledge of the team and add it to your own. In the case of reaching an agreement, it's the foundation of lasting relationships that won't later be ruptured by objections not being heard. This is extremely important. Autocratic leadership is unwelcome and will not survive for long. It is a corrosive and unsustainable leadership style.

Creating rapport

When someone begins to enjoy your company, it becomes much easier to enlist their support. This makes it more likely that they'll support your viewpoint in situations that count. Allies are people who like and trust you. Your relationships are what will move your goals forward and create a foundation for your success - and that of your allies, as well. People, while perhaps not being entirely aware of this on an intellectual level, know this instinctively. That is why you must prioritize establishing rapport with others. It's the basis of strong allegiances.

Part of creating rapport is establishing the common interests you hold with others. Taking an interest in them and offering them information about who you are is how this can be achieved. Being too veiled about yourself makes you appear cold, calculating, and detached. Establish that you're open and a person who can be trusted.

It's also important to establish rapport with others and one way this can be done is to mirror their body language. You'll probably find, if you pay attention, that you do this anyway when as begun to relate to someone. Mirroring body language sends the unconscious signal that there is a bond already established between two people and they're on the same team. Mirroring speech patterns is another way of doing this. Repeating keywords with enthusiasm at opportune times is the natural way we tell each other that we're enjoying a conversation or agreeing with each other. Nod, smile, and respond positively when you sense a common theme emerging in conversation. This sends the message that you're accessible on the most basic human level.

Suggestions instead of demands

People routinely bridle at strong directives. In Western societies, where individualism is a way of life, we like to believe in our autonomy as a value. That means it's not the best course of action to demand things from people. Much more effective is suggesting a course of action and building a consensus based on suggestion, while being open to input and concessions to other points of view. This is the democratic way of achieving goals and one that is completely manageable through the application of a deft hand.

Here are examples of language that gives your listener the option to chip in and yet still leaves you the "wiggle room" to get to where you believe you need to go:

- Would you be interested in doing a-b-c?
- Could you be interested in doing a-b-c?
- I think we should do a-b-c. What do you think?
- Do you think this is the best way forward, or do you have other ideas?

Leaving space for opinion and input, while still advancing the validity of your opinion, is the stuff of which influence is made. While you're providing people with a rationale for your point of view, your willingness to entertain amendments to that point of view only increases your influential power. Imposition of one's opinion rarely ends in anything but resentment. By building a consensus through input and exchange, you will still arrive at the goal you have in mind, but you'll do it with the support of a willing team that signs on to the plan in question. A fringe benefit? That input will undoubtedly improve on the original plan and could result in satisfaction on the part of all involved.

Heightening your awareness

Awareness of the responses of others to what you're saying is a key to influential action. What are their facial expressions telling you? Their body language and word choices? What about tone and pitch? All these factors are rich with information that you can draw upon to temper your pitch and get people on your side. It can also cue you to back off and change lanes, while you re-group and allow others their input.

Active listening, while employing body language (head nodding, eye contact) and assenting noises ("uh-huh", "yes", "I see") is also about deeply engaging with what's being said and any complimentary messages being sent by the speaker. Your awareness in crucial situations, of all the factors that create a communicative environment, is of the utmost importance. You need to be aware, not only of what's being said, but also implications of what's intended - what's not being said and the speaker's frame of mind. All these factors work together to form a more concise body of information upon which you may draw to apply influential action.

Conclusion

You will agree with the assessment that manipulation is everywhere in our daily lives. Even while you sleep, there is a brand out there somewhere looking to unleash their marketing campaign to make you spend your money. While you slave away at work at the mercy of your boss, there is no guarantee that you will get a promotion. In your relationships, there is probably someone pretending to be your friend who is only looking out for themself It seems like whichever way you turn, someone is waiting to influence your next move. This can be quite overwhelming.

Being manipulated does not feel good. Knowing that everything you thought was true was an altered reality created by a manipulative person makes you feel betrayed and, oftentimes, stupid. You wonder why you did not see the red flags and what you could have done differently. The truth of the matter is that however smart you think you are, there is always someone who believes they can outsmart you. Enter your new manipulation methods.

You do not have to sit back and watch other people take control and get what they want when you can do it yourself. Influencing other people into fulfilling your desires is well within your reach if you internalize and incorporate the teachings and methods in this book. It might seem like an uphill climb, especially if you are used to giving other people what they want and getting nothing in return, but it is not. Learning how to manipulate people is not something that should overwhelm you. It only feels overwhelming now because you are learning all these new things all at once. With time and practice, what you have learned will become second nature. You will find yourself smiling and flirting without even thinking about it.

Start the work from within: working on your body language, presentation, communication techniques and then apply the outcome to the external environment. You will be surprised how much more you gain from people and the world around you if you subtly manipulate them. Becoming a master manipulator will take longer than a few days, but it will be worth the work and the wait. Remember, as long as you are not hurting anyone, who does not deserve to be hurt, you are well within your rights to manipulate your way to the success you have always envisioned for yourself!

Body Language

Reading Minds Through Body Language - Change how People See You

Axel Scott

Introduction

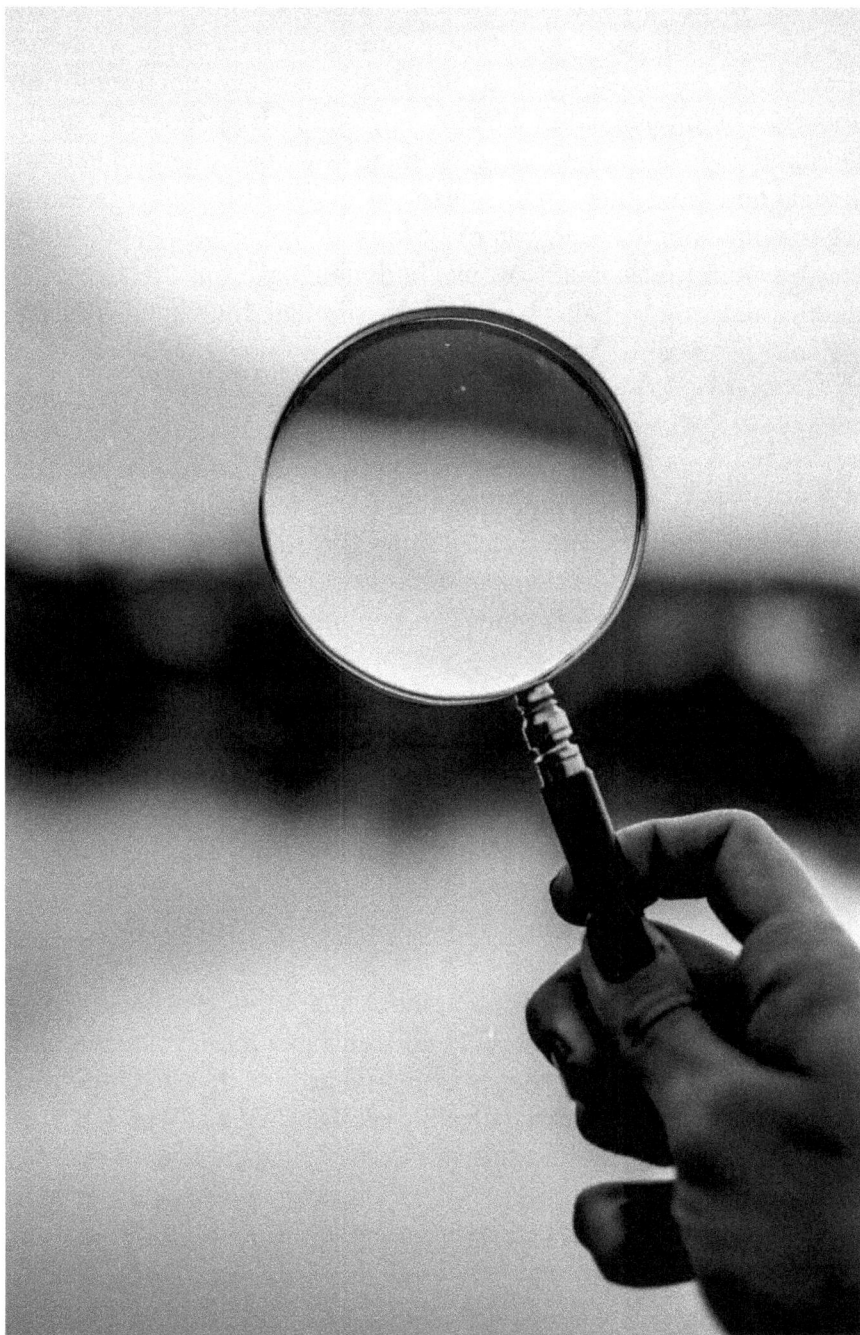

Body language points to the nonverbal cues used by humans to have effective communication with each other. Such nonverbal signals, according to scholars, constitute a significant part of daily interaction. It has also been reported that body language can account for about 60 to 65 percent of all communication. It is necessary to understand body language, and it is vital to pay close attention to other signals and what they might mean. In many situations, instead of relying on a single event, you must look at signals as a band. When you learn and master how to use body language for effective communication, you will also be able to manipulate individuals psychologically in a positive manner.

What Is Body Language?
Even when they don't express their opinions verbally, the majority still miss clues about what they think and feel. Nonverbal signals transmitted through the formation of the sender's body, physical appearance, voice inflections, and intensity of the voice, and various signs are all referred to as nonverbal communication.

Nonverbal communication is usually not as simple as it is conveyed in words, but how it is expressed could take on a major job by recognizing somebody and interfacing with others. It's a quiet ensemble: mini-expressions (short presentations of feeling that individual attempts to disguise), hand gestures, and the recording of posture in the human mind very rapidly in any event, when someone is not consciously aware of them.

However short, these acknowledgment snapshots can have lasting repercussions on how an individual translates the inspiration, disposition, and receptivity of others as well as how they see their own inner identity. Regrettably, certain psychological well-being issues, particularly neuropsychiatric issues such as mental defects, may make it even more trying to test to recognize and respond to nonverbal communication messages.

Types of Body Language

There are types of body language. This is because we cannot classify the different styles in the same category. Body languages can be distinguished and classified. So, which body language styles can be differentiated? Generally, the body language is divided into two columns. That includes; Body parts and the Intent.

So what kinds in each class can be observed?

Let us start with the body parts and the language they communicate.

The Head - The head's placement and its movement, back and forth, right to left, side to side, and the shake of hair

Face - This includes facial expressions. You should note that the face has many muscles ranging from 54 to 98, whose work is to move different areas of the face. The movements of the face depict the state of your mind.

Eyebrows - The eyebrows can express themselves through moving up and down, as well as frowning.

Eyes - The eyes can be rolled, moved up and down, right and left, blink, and dilate.

The Nose - The nose's expression can be by the flaring of the nostrils and the formation of wrinkles at the top by scrunching up the nose.

The Lips - There are many roles played by the lips; they include snarling, smiling, kissing, opening, closing, and puckering

The Tongue - The tongue can roll in and out, go up and down, touch while kissing, and can also lick the lips.

The Jaw - The jaw opens and closes. It can be clenched, and the lower jaw can be moved right and left as well.

Your Body Posture - This describes how you place your body, legs, and arms altogether, especially in relation to other people.

The Body Proximity - This looks at how far or near your body is to other people.

Shoulder Movements - They move up and down, get hunched, and hung.

The Arm - These go up and down, straight and cross

The Legs and feet - These can have an expression in many different ways. They can be straight, crossed, one leg placed over the other, the feet facing the next person you are in a conversation with or face away from each other, the feet can be dangling the shoes, and so on.

The hand and the fingers - The way the hands and fingers move usually helps to read people's gestures. The hands can move up and down or can be used to send signals (secret messages) that can be deciphered by those who know the code.

Handling and placing of objects -This is not regarded as a body part, but it technically plays a role in reading body language. This may predict anger, happiness, and much more.

Moreover, this includes willingly making body movements, otherwise known as gestures. They are the movements that you intend to make. For example, shaking of hands, blinking of the eyes, moving and shaking the body in a sexy way, maybe to lure someone, and much more.

There are also involuntary movements- the movements that you have no control over. It can be sweating, laughter, crying, and much more.

Chapter 1:
Body Language origin and the Science Behind It

If you've ever been to another country, you're sure to realize that some of the body languages you use at home will be translated differently. This's because there're cultural differences between America and the country you're visiting, and each group of people is going to see things in a slightly different way.

The differences that show up in various cultures are also going to be present in many different circumstances. This might simply include interactions that occur between different genders, the interactions that occur between those of the same gender, the conversational distance that you should have with people, and how much physical touch should be allowed in the conversation. For example, some cultures feel that physical touch is expressive; hence it is used a lot. You'll be able to find this in places such as Italy, where a kiss on each cheek and a big hug is considered acceptable and even common when it comes to greetings. On the other hand, when you're in Japan, you'll find that a proper greeting is going to include a respectful bow, and there'll be no touch at all.

Comfort distances and personal space are often influenced by the culture that you live in or are visiting. For example, those from South America will see that their comfort distances and personal space tend to be a lot smaller than in other cultures. People from these countries will stand close to each other when they're talking; it doesn't matter whether they know each other that well or not. On the other hand, people in the United States also value a larger personal space, and they're not that comfortable when others stand too close, especially when the other person isn't a familiar face.

These kinds of cultural differences that are found in body language are often going to be the most pronounced when it comes to gender interactions. A lot of cultures still see the man as the dominant gender and assume the male to be of higher status than the female. Often, the body language that's used in these interactions will be reflected from this viewpoint. You may find in some cultures that women are required to avert their eyes when they're in the presence of a man, or they might be required to walk a few steps behind any male they're with. On the other hand, in western cultures, you'll find that gender expectations have changed, and this allows men and women to share a more equal status when it comes to acceptable

110

body language.

You may wonder why these differences in cultural body language are going to be so important. These differences are a direct result of how the culture thinks and acts, and so you'll be able to learn a lot about that culture by the body language exhibited. If you're planning to visit an unfamiliar country, whether for pleasure or business, it's often necessary to understand the body language they value to lessen or prevent the cultural shock. Displaying the wrong kind of body language could land you in a lot of trouble with people who're unfamiliar with this style of behavior. For example, if you're on a trip for business and use the wrong kind of body language, you can send out messages that will hurt the deal you're trying to make fast. In the world of traveling for pleasure, the wrong kind of body language is going to lead to hostile and sometimes dangerous situations.

A good example of this is in the Middle East. In this scenario, a male businessperson is going to have much more leeway in the manner that he conducts business there as well as where he's able to walk. There's also more access to local business opportunities at many different levels. This is in comparison to women, most of whom aren't able to do business in this area due to the cultural aversion to interacting with women, which is often too much to overcome, so most businesses will avoid that.

If you're planning on going on a vacation to a country with a different culture, it might be a good idea to pay some attention to the body language that's expected in that area to understand what's going on better and help you avoid any problems that may arise. For instance, if you happen to get lost in Japan, you're more likely to receive some help from a citizen there if you're able to show some respectful body language and then follow the local customs such as avoiding touch and perhaps respecting that you bow when you ask for help. If you're rude or don't follow customs, it might be difficult to get the kind of help that you need.

There are a lot of different things that you can consider when you're looking at body language in the United States compared to other countries. Some of these would include:

Eye contact – In the U.S. and Canada, intermittent eye contact is very important to show that you're interested and paying attention to the other person. On the other hand, in a lot of the cultures of the Middle East, intense eye contact that's shared between those of the same gender is a symbol of sincerity and trust, while eye contact that occurs between those of opposite genders, especially when it comes Muslim cultures, anything longer than a brief eye contact is going to be seen as inappropriate. Also, Latin American, African and Asian cultures are going to see extended eye contact as a challenge, and the Japanese see even a little bit of eye contact as something uncomfortable. In some other cultures, it's expected that a woman looks down when she's talking to a man.

Handshakes – In Western cultures, it's acceptable to shake hands as a form of greeting another person when you're meeting up. In other cultures, there're quite a few differences that might surprise you. For example, a lot of northern European cultures will also use a firm one pump handshake as a greeting, while parts of South America, Central America, and Southern Europe will use a longer handshake that's considered warmer; this means that they'll take the left hand and use it to clasp the hand, elbow, and sometimes the lapel of the other person. You should be careful with handshakes in Turkey; this gesture is often considered aggressive and rude. In some African countries, a limp form of a handshake is the norm. In Islamic countries, a man will also never shake the hand of a woman who's not a part of his family.

Greetings – In America, there're many different types of standard greetings that can be used, and these have been engraved into many from childhood. But these kinds of greetings aren't going to be found everywhere that you look and sometimes you might confuse another culture by using them abroad. For example, if you're in Japan, you'll be expected to bow to those you're greeting, while in Italy, you'd give people kisses on the cheek.

Personal Space – This was mentioned briefly above, but each culture is also going to have a different meaning for personal space. In America, personal space is valued, and most people don't want to have others too close to them, especially if they've just met. In China, those who're doing business together wouldn't find it acceptable to have any personal space at all. Strangers are going to touch often when they're in crowded meetings.

Touching – Touching is another thing that's going to vary depending on the country you're in. While touching is fine in America, many cultures would have rules on how this should take place. In countries that are Islamic, a man is only allowed ever to touch his wife. In England, Scandinavia and Japan, touching isn't that frequent. Latino cultures go the opposite route in that touching is often encouraged. Most of the time, it's best to follow the lead of the natives when visiting other countries. Let the other people guide you a bit, and soon you'll be able to determine what behavior is appropriate. Certain countries don't encourage touching the heads of children, for example, so steer clear of this unless you're sure it's acceptable.

Personal hygiene and dress – About the only common across cultures is that brushing of teeth is usually normal practice. Otherwise, there're a lot of differences that you'll find as you travel. In some cultures, women aren't expected to shave. Some cultures are never going to wear deodorant and might not reserve as much time for bathing. You must make sure that when you're going to another country that you aren't offending anyone or that you don't easily get offended.

Gestures – The gestures that you make with your hands are also going to mean different things in various parts of the world. You may find that avoiding these gestures is the best bet when you're in another country. If you were to use a rude hand gesture toward someone in one country, they may not realize what you're doing and won't get offended because it has no meaning in their country. In some cultures, the middle finger is going to be used as the pointer finger, so they'll not translate it as an insult. The thumbs-up signal is often different as well. Other signs that you should watch out for would include the okay sign and placing your hands on your hips. If you aren't sure that they'll be recognized as polite, then it's best to avoid using them.

The thing to remember about this is that when it comes to the differences in body language culturally, it's important to have a little bit of knowledge ahead of time. This will allow you to understand what's expected of you so that you can enjoy your experience in the new country without causing any issues for the citizens who live there and yourself.

Chapter 2:
The Psychology Behind Body Language

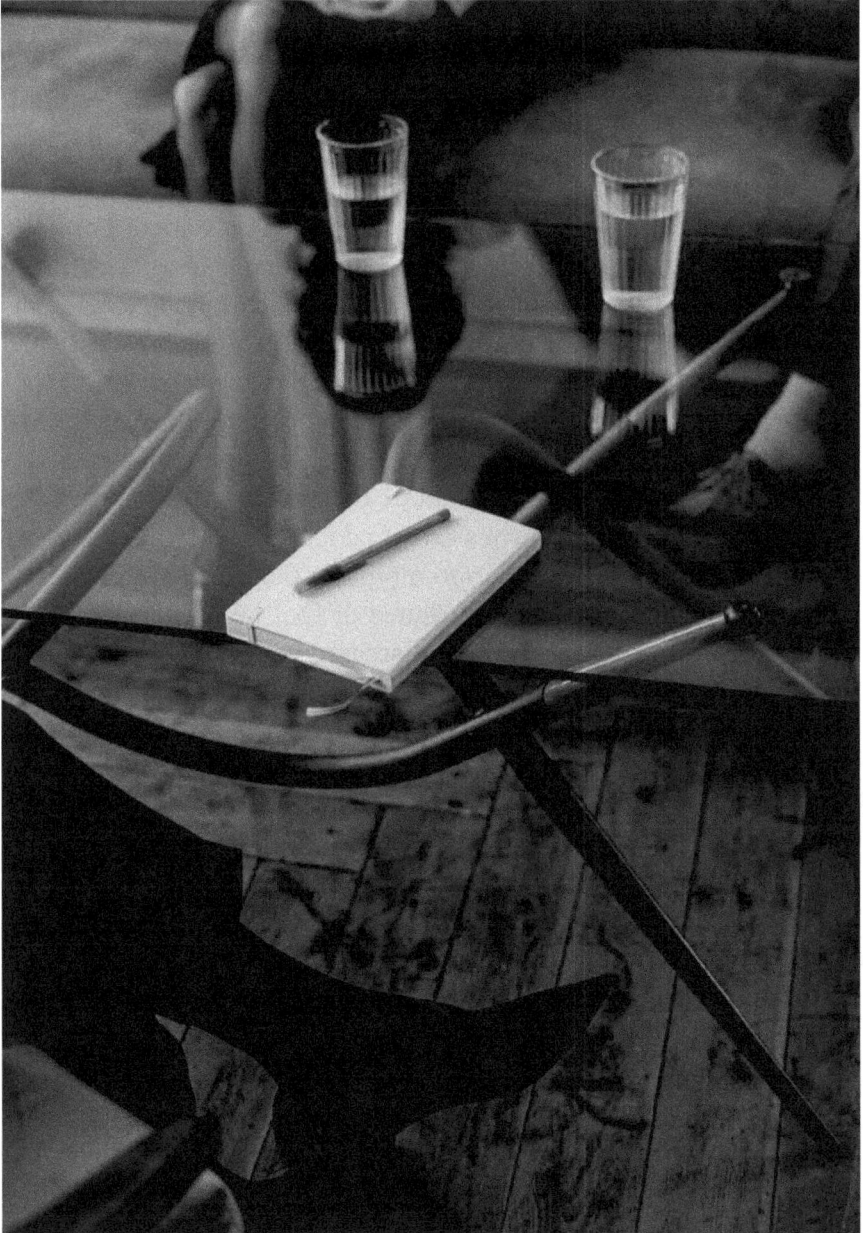

Regardless of how great you get at perusing nonverbal communication, you may never feel that you have idealized it since this is such an immense subject. Nonetheless, a couple of essentials will consistently enable you to get a reasonable idea of what is happening. This, as a matter of first importance, is the ability that you'll have to create, which is a sharp perception. You need to begin searching for the indications. However, this must be done normally and pair with your verbal correspondence, except if you need to crack the other individual out totally. The indications are:

- Inconsistencies – Is the body language in a state of harmony with the verbal language? Is the individual saying "yes" while the body is stating "no"? Nonverbal correspondence assembled–one single motion may not mean so much excessively. Try not to peruse a lot there. Or maybe, focus on a bunch of actions when gathering signals that are sent–like the tone of the voice, outward appearance, eye development, hands development, and so on. What do they say together?

- Check out your hunches–Most people "know" what the other says. You will have that premonition that this individual isn't coming clean, or isn't intrigued or that he is engrossed with something different–don't disregard your hunch because the individual is stating the inverse too articulately. Know and be increasingly cautious when your hunch is sending you cautioning signals. Watch intently for body language that does not coordinate with their words.

- Eye contact– Is the eye-to-eye connection without flaw? Or then again, is it subtle or excessively exceptional?

- Facial appearance–Is the face responsive? Is it a cover for lack of interest? Is it hard and unforgiving? Is it vivified with intrigue? Does it coordinate the words?

- The tone of the voice–There are 1001 different ways to state "come here" or "bless your heart." Attempt it. Let's assume it is said with shock, outrage, pity, enthusiasm, bliss, etc. The manner of speaking can disclose your bounty. Do you discover warmth there or frigidity? Is it stressed? Is it sure or bashful? Is it trying or empowering? Here and there, a simple "how do you do?" could establish the tone of the dialog.

- The posture of the body and motions–Investigate how the individual is holding his body. Is it firm and antagonistic? Is it the "I'm into you" type? Is it slumped and sad? Is it tense? Are shoulders unbending and raised? Is the chest area turned one side while the feet are on another? Are the hands motions inside the body edge or move much outward?
- Touch–Is there contact? If there is, is it proper? Is the individual attacking your well-being zone? Is the contact commanding or agreeable? Does it make you feel better, disturb you, or fill you with fear?
- The intensity of the character–Is the individual excessively sensational? Excessively calm? Excessively cold? Excessively risky? Excessively level?
- Timing and pace of the discussion/exchange–Is the verbal communication too quick that it looks restless? Or, on the other hand, too moderate that it looks uninterested? Do the nonverbal sign stay aware of the words–or is the mouth saying one thing and the body language another? All these are signals that will disclose to you what the other individual is thinking and intending to do. The capacity to peruse it precisely would enable you to acquire the activity and intercede in such a way that you get the activity you need from the individual you are conversing with. It is tied in with getting your direction.
- Outward appearance–In many cases, what you think and feel is reflected in your face. A few people ace the craftsmanship of keeping a clear face, yet that would be temporarily similar to when seeming a meeting or betting–and this would be to anticipate the other individual and read what the genuine sentiments are.

Six fundamental appearances are basic to the human species and can be examined the same everywhere throughout the world:
- Anger- You will know from the facial expression of the individual that he is irate. There is a scowl; eyelids become limited, lips are tight and frequently in a straight line, and nostrils flare.

- Appall- The nose wrinkles in a disgusting manner, and the face folds–eyebrows descend, and cheek muscles are pulled up.
- Fear- The outward appearance of dread is all-inclusive. Eyes augment, the mouth opens in a wheezing signal, cheek muscles get tense, and eyebrows shoot up, wrinkling the brow.
- Satisfaction- Smiling is the first and most basic outward appearance that says, "I'm upbeat." The face is loose, inviting, and warm. Wrinkles are framed at the side of the eyes– snicker lines.
- Trouble- You will find that the corners of the eyebrow go marginally up, lips' corners descend (tragic smiley or emoji) at some point, they quiver declaring, tears. Tears are additionally an indication of misery (likewise of extreme satisfaction).
- Shock. Jaw drops, eyebrows shoot up, and eyes enlarge. Wrinkles would be shaped in the brow, and the mouth drops open.

Furthermore, some all-inclusive and simple to read articulations are a lot more mixed and changes. The eyes are the most "loquacious" in their outward appearances. Other than demonstrating these essential articulations/feelings, there are:

- Feeling uncomfortable–Sideways looking, subtle looking, dashing eye-to-eye connection, looking down, looking nervously around the room, or towards the entryway may pass on this. An excessive amount of flickering likewise can be taken as an indication of anxiety.
- Lying–Subtle looks, failure to keep up watchful gaze contact, taking a gander at hands could signify that the individual isn't coming clean.
- Giving space–Is utilized in jam-packed spots where eye-to-eye connection could end up overpowering. You would encounter this look in lifts, trams, railroad stations, air terminals, and so on where you are in a group.

- Deference–In numerous societies, someone "looking straight without flinching" is viewed as a proud and testing specialist. Thus, those with lesser rank would lower their eyes when tending to somebody of a higher position. In some cultures, ladies are expected to look down as an affirmation of unobtrusiveness. Ladies who lookup would be seen as "having a loose character" or "requesting sex" in specific parts of the world.
- Dominance–You'd have known about the phrase, "gazing him down." This is the point at which the eyes are exhausting and courageous, compelling the other individual to break eye contact first. This is a commanding look and is utilized typically by one who either accepts he is higher in rank or needs to threaten others into accepting that. For instance, how an individual carries his body says a ton regarding what the individual feels. A shy individual will conduct himself uniquely in contrast to how a certain and confident individual does.
- Nervous, hesitant, low confidence–The body is slumped, bears down in a practically recoiling stance, head twisted forward, eyes looking down or darting quickly around, legs either crossed firmly or with feet extremely near one another, arms covering the defenseless zone of the body (neck, tummy catch level and crotch). It says, "Let me out of here. I'm not comfortable here."
- Dominant, brimming with certainty, pioneer–Body upstanding, jaw pushed forward, head tilted upwards, incredible step, feet at shoulder's width or marginally more, hands along the edge and outward, chest puffed, shoulders squared, hands moving inside the body width with exact developments, eyes full contact, checking you.
- Arrogant, grandiose, full of himself–Body taking more space than required, head tilted in reverse, eyes testing, feet wide separated, hands signal noisy, energetic and wide, crotch uncovered improperly, eyes pushing you into the ground.

- Arm Position - How you hold your arms opposite your body will likewise enlighten you a great deal regarding what you feel and think. In general, individuals will make self-defensive motions when they are not happy with what they see, hear, or feel. Whenever agreeable and pleasant, they enable themselves to be uncovered and open.
- Uncomfortable, untrusting, shut—The arms and hands will attempt to cover the body's powerless parts, for example, the arms touching the neck divide, round the belly button, or in the lap covering the crotch territory. You may likewise discover the arms crossed on the chest.
- Trusting, intrigued, open—The arms of the individual who is intrigued, open, and trusting would have the body open to you with arms by his side or expressively motioning with them.
- Space Zones— Space isn't nonverbal communication; however, it is a significant factor. The space one makes around himself can demonstrate reasonably precisely how they are feeling. There are four sorts of zones. They are; the open zone, the social zone, the individual zone, and the cozy zone.
➢ The Public Zone (About 12 feet from some other individual)— This is commonly the separation one puts between himself and an open speaker. This is non-threatening and non-attacking. It is additionally a zone where there is almost no dedication between the speaker and the audience.
➢ The Social Zone— This is a separation of 4-12 feet and would characterize the space put between us and the those we know, however, not very well. The clerk, the copier machine administrator, etc. In this zone are individuals who you don't permit to get to your private emotions; in any case, in this zone, there is a level of amicability and solace.
➢ The Personal zone—This covers a separation of 1½ - 4 feet around us. This is where we permit individuals when connecting in open places, for example, eateries, workplace, parties, and so forth

➢ The Intimate Zone–This is around 18 creeps to contacting separation, and in this circle/zone, we permit just those we trust totally. When you discover outsiders in this space, it makes you awkward. This is why we feel swarmed in small places, for example, lifts, trains, and so on, and individuals keep away from eye contact.

As should be obvious, the intricacies of body language can fill volumes. In any case, we are not here to peruse volumes of scholarly stuff on what body language shows. We can leave that for researchers and scholars. What we have to know is how to utilize it in our everyday lives to improve our connections at work and home.

Chapter 3:
Verbal and Nonverbal Communication

It is generally believed that communication is a fundamental part of human behavior, but now, it is becoming evident that many communication channels happen through nonverbal means. You look at someone and get the message they are passing across, you see a woman snap her fingers, and you get the message or an idea of what she's trying to say. It is a social infusion of interaction with a basic context of information flowing through knowledge in the human habit. It activates the passing of information or messages to an extent where interpretation is needed to prove the coherence of such a message. Communication occurs after signals move from one channel to another, carrying information-related content between a sender and a receiver through a communication chain. As much as language is needed for communication to have a balanced substance in precision, it is important to understand the message in between. Language strengthens the communication system and allows humans to choose their words or signals in the generality of coded signals. Meanwhile, there is a seeming connection between what is said and what is heard. And at times, there is no need for words, which is why nonverbal means of communication are in vogue too. Communication as an aspect of social life must come with meaningful information as no message is passed when there is no meaning to it. This now serves as fundamental leverage of words, how meanings are conveyed in the right manner and how they are conceived. You should also note that there are messages whose meanings aren't what you'd get immediately but certainly later. So it boils down to getting acquainted with some basic communication tools and setting your baseline right so you can get the meanings or insight of the message when it surfaces. As a good listener who is willing to analyze people, you should always try as much as possible to understand and perceive when words are connotative or denotative. This idea gives you a balance in your presumption, and with that, you're able to decide whether a particular message has a meaning or not. In the process of communication, there is encoding from the speaker, who presumes you, as a listener, would grasp the intents of his message.

To get the scope of communication and its proper analysis, you as a speaker should always consider the perspective of your co-participant. Creating a bridge of understanding before formulating your message goes a long way in ensuring a mutual understanding of the subject.

Verbal Communication

Communication systems employ the signs and symbols for interaction purposes.

Signs are signals used to convey a message, so also is the general philosophy of verbal communication. Getting the whole idea of verbal communication and translating them rightly is a function of the receiver knowing the cause of the action. How do I mean? You get to understand a particular signal because you understand the cause of the action. For example, if your child mutters some words and points directly at the door, what does that mean? It means that probably someone is at the door or attention is needed at the door. On the other hand, symbols indicate a complex level of reasoning and understanding between the parties involved. Symbols, as complex as they seem, bring about the concept of symbolic interactions theory.

Whenever verbal communication takes place, it allows us to look for and understand the symbolic content that gives us the idea of what the speaker is talking about. This process is sub-divided into:

SEMANTICITY: A semanticist knows the relationship between the after-effect of action and what causes it. As you know that signals stand for a particular meaning of their own even though they might be construed to mean other complex things. For example, a little child shouting at the top of his voice with a sharp knife in his hand connotes something. So as an observer, what comes to mind is that he cut himself with the knife and not that his noise stands out rightly for the cut itself. It allows you to see occurrences differently as much as you see them separately to understand the main message it's passing across.

GENERATIVITY: Generativity takes the stand that a finite message could take the shape of infinite meanings. The idea shows the level at which diverse thoughts range from individual to individual. And that's why languages can combine and recombine symbols and signals to produce meaningful and comprehensible utterances to users of the language.

DISPLACEMENT: This third pillar supports the idea of communicating what is abstract, and it has a linkage in language. This is because the language gives room for the communication of things that only mentally exist. Through this displacement factor, the imaginative tendencies allow communicating participants to discuss what only exists in the imagination aside from what can be seen.

Body Language

Irrespective of where you find yourself, as much as information and message are concerned, body language is also essential. Of all we communicate, there is a belief that body language takes over 65 percent of what we communicate, so understanding people's nonverbal cues is a priceless tool.

Learning How To Read Body Language

Understanding people around you is a valuable skill, hence learning more about how to read body language. Doing this can save you or people around you in time of distress; why? Because you're able to get the body language a person gives you, which means he/she can communicate if there is or they are in danger as soon as possible when speech is impossible. The following tips are how to learn some common body language cues which you'll find interesting to know.

Studying the Eyes

The eye's language tells more, which is why you must pay close attention when communicating with someone. Making direct eye contact or looking away from both means a lot in communication. As direct eye contact means having an interest in what one is gazing at, or sincerity, inability to make eye contact results in the opposite, which indicates disinterest and boredom, especially when someone is looking away, which sometimes connotes guilt or deceit.

Dilated pupils are also one of the cues you should watch out for to determine if someone is responding to you positively. You automatically get an idea of what someone feels about you when the eyes dilate, which signifies their interest. Though very hard to detect, but you can get it right when you carefully focus on the present situation that instigated it. Glancing and blinking rate and the way they are done also go a long way in suggesting the sensation, desire for a thing, or imagination in interpersonal social cues.

Gaze at the Face –Touching Mouth or Smiling-
Even though people can influence and easily change their facial expressions, it is still easier to detect when seen from the right angle. While smiling is an everyday cue, it shouldn't be misconstrued every time as the normal meaning it bears.
Smiling is the best body signal, but smiles could be interpreted in several ways. Smiles can be genuine, or they might be used to show cynicism, sarcasm, or false happiness. Always take note of the genuine smiles (engaging the whole face), the fake ones (uses only the mouth), and the ones that mean other gestures (other parts of the face or the eyes). Also, take note of the half-smile as this is another facial expression to look out for, which at times means uncertainty or sarcasm.

Paying close attention to the distance
Doing this is called proximity. At times you get an idea of what a person is trying to say when you understand their closeness or distance to you. So when you're with someone, you must pay attention to this proximity and the ideas surrounding it. You can get a feeling of someone else when they sit beside you. So when someone sits very close to you or far away, you tend to know their seeming intentions towards you. Also, some signals come with proximity, allowing you to determine if there would be a sort of rapport between you and someone else.

Check for mirroring
When someone mimics you, be sure it has a meaning as body language. Mirroring has to do with mimicking the other person's body language. However, it is essential to note that the other person in your communication channel mirrors your signals and body lan-

guage. So try changing your posture consistently to see if someone closer to you does the same. This is a signal that such a person is trying to create a kind of friendship tie with you for that moment. You could try this in a public setting and good results.

Observe the head movements well

Whenever you are with someone, always check and observe the rate at which the person's head moves. For instance, when you have chit-chat with someone, and he or she slowly nods his head, it is a sign of approval or interest in the subject you're discussing. While a fast nodding reveals that the person in question has had much information from you, which is cool, observe when someone tilts his head backward. This can be a sign of suspicion and uncertainty about what you're saying. Tilting the head sideways can be referred to as a sign of interest as well. Getting to know all these things gives you a clearer clue about what someone thinks about you in any social relationship.

The Feet and Hands Are A Selling Point

People unconsciously reveal more than they would ordinarily let out in conversations through the feet. Most times, people place more concentration on the upper part of the body in conversations or meetings, whereas more than enough details of their intentions are leaking through their feet. So through this body language, you can easily tell if someone in a discussion is interested in you and what you are saying when their feet point towards you. When otherwise, be sure that the person will soon take his leave towards his feet's direction. The best application of this strategy is in a group discussion or meeting where people show their minds through their faces; you can easily tell which are still interested in the conversation this way. The same thing goes with the hands too. In a conversation, someone might put one or both hands in his pocket; these two have meanings. While the former could mean that he is confident talking to you, the latter shows a bit of concern about what you're talking about.

Chapter 4:
Basic Techniques to Easily Improve Your Body Language

There's no definitive advice on using body language because interpretation depends on the setting, situation, and cultural context. The way you use body language when talking to your mother compared to when you talk to your boss or a person you're intensely attracted to differs from each other. There are simple ways that can help you communicate effectively with your body.

1. Be aware of your body. Simply observe yourself—How you sit, stand, and walk, use your arms, legs, and hands, and what your body does while talking to someone you know, for example. You may already be aware of some of your mannerisms and particular bodily quirks, like biting your nails when nervous or pinching your nose when upset, or just twirling your hair when with someone you like, but you may be surprised to discover new ones. A lot of these quirks, mannerisms, and knee jerk reactions we cannot control, but when we're aware of them, we understand why we do them.

2. Maintain steady eye contact, but don't stare for too long. Eye contact is like a requirement when talking to someone, but the intensity and frequency of eye contact also depend heavily on your relationship with the person you're talking to, the setting or context, and the nature of your conversation.

    For some people, prolonged eye contact and being stared at makes them uncomfortable or creeps them out. On the flip side, if you don't maintain eye contact, you'll also more likely come across as insecure, timid, hiding something, or insincere. What's the best thing to do then? If you're talking to several people, give some time to make eye contact with all of them to establish connections and gauge whether they're listening to you and are interested. If talking with one person, find that balance between maintaining eye contact at the most crucial points of the conversation and looking away every once in a while. That way, the other person will also know that you're still interested in the conversation and won't feel offended by your gaze.

3. Sit and stand up straighter. How many times have we been told to sit or stand up straight and not slouch? More often than not, a slouched posture is immediately associated with a lack of confidence. You wouldn't want to give away that kind of impression, especially during a job interview or a first date. Whatever situation you find yourself in, it's always better to be aware of your stance and posture and fix it when you find yourself slouching. Keep your back and head straight, your spine aligned, and your shoulders level.

4. Keep your head up. Like a slouched posture, just keeping your eyes down on the ground is also associated with insecurity and lack of confidence. Keep your chin up, with your head straight and your eyes looking straight ahead.

5. Don't be afraid to take up some space. Simply taking up a bit of space by sitting or standing with your legs apart is a sign of having self-confidence and being comfortable in your skin. Don't worry about offending other people's sense of personal space, though. It's all still within the acceptable bounds of personal space as long as you don't bump or graze into someone in the process.

6. Relax your shoulders. When you're tense, it's also most obvious in the way your shoulders hunch up or down. Try to relax and lose a bit of the tension by pulling your shoulders back and shaking them slightly. Also, leaning back slightly makes you look confident and at ease.

7. Avoid crossing your arms and legs. That is if you don't want to be perceived as defensive, guarded, or insecure in business and social gatherings or situations.

8. Give indications of interest in conversations. Nod, smile, laugh, lean your head to the side, and react appropriately during conversations. Insert sounds that indicate interest or agreement like "uh-huh," "yeah," or "okay." Also, showing positive signals encourage people to listen and pay attention to you. Otherwise, the other person will unequivocally conclude that you aren't interested at all. Be careful not to overdo it, though, so as not to seem overeager or needy for approval.

9. Slow down your movements. This is helpful, especially when you're feeling nervous, uncomfortable, or shy. Deliberately slowing your movements, like just walking slowly, can make you look more at ease with yourself, calm, and confident.

10. Eliminate or minimize distracting movements. As much as possible, try to be conscious of and avoid distracting mannerisms like fidgeting in your seat when you're nervous, drumming your fingers on a surface when impatient, touching your face when you're flustered, or shaking your legs back and forth. Body movements such as these are not only distracting to others but indicate your level of discomfort.

11. Be aware of others' personal space. As a general rule, don't stand too close when talking to someone you aren't close with on a personal level. Especially at work and other professional settings, boundaries are always expected to be given respect and consideration.

12. Always maintain a positive attitude. No matter what kind of situation you find yourself in, try to always keep a cool and positive attitude. Strive to be relaxed and open. How you're feeling inside will always be expressed in your body language, if not in words you speak.

13. Learn to manage stress. Stress somehow messes up your physical, emotional, and mental well-being. It even compromises your ability to communicate well. The more you're stressed out, the more likely you are to misread people and send confusing mismatched signals. If you're feeling overwhelmed by stress, just take a moment to calm down before joining the conversation again. Once you feel more at ease, you can better deal with the situation or conversation you're involved in.

Chapter 5:
Body Language Myths You Should Know About

Your face is only one small part of your body, but it has a massive impact on what people will be able to pick up from you. While your face might occupy a relatively small portion of your body, it's still an important part that can express a lot of very crucial signals to the person that you're communicating with. It is the most popular part of our body. The face is what people are introduced to even before knowing your name. They want to look in your eyes, at your mouth and get a better understanding of what you're trying to share. Let's take a look at all the ways that your facial expressions can share greater truth about you.

Microexpressions
Microexpressions are tiny little features within our face that give us a better indication of what somebody else might be thinking or wanting to do. Whether it's a small wrinkle in the forehead or how the mouth is moved, we can start to pick up on these tiny microexpressions to better understand what somebody is thinking.

There are seven different emotions that we can pick up through microexpressions. These include anger, fear, disgust, sadness, content, happiness, and surprise.

These microexpressions will be expressed in different ways by different people. However, there are specific indications that we can use, which will help us better understand what somebody might be feeling.

Anger— It is something that we can pick up on by how a person uses their eyebrows and their mouth.

If eyebrows are pointed down and inwards towards the nose, then this is a sign of anger. The lower lid might also become raised and closing over their eyes in a way that makes the eyes look a little bit more squinted. They'll often keep their lips sucked in and tighten the muscles around their mouths.

They might have a frown in the tenseness of the cheeks and in the mouth pointing downwards.

Disgust—We can show disgust in the same way we do anger in terms of eyebrow usage. Disgust will often leave the person with their mouth hanging open a little bit more. They'll have tense cheeks and a wrinkled nose. Their face is recoiling away from the disgusting thing that they're hearing.

Fear—Fear is going to have similar eyebrow movements as well. However, they'll be raised extremely high and flat.

If somebody's forehead is wrinkled, and their mouth is slightly open, this can tell us that they are feeling fear. Look at the rest of their body to be sure if it's fear or just surprise.

Surprise— It looks a lot like fear but a little bit more positively. When somebody is surprised, they'll have curved eyebrows versus flat eyebrows as when they're fearful. They'll have their mouth open, but they might have the corners of their mouth turned up a little bit as well.

Sadness— Even when we receive bad news, we can still sometimes have a smile. The smile might manifest simply because we're trying to work through our emotions. Sadness is like anger turned downwards. You'll have those arched eyebrows, except they'll be hanging a little bit looser and closer to your eyes.

A more relaxed cheek is seen in sadness, but the corners of the mouth will also be turned down.

Content— This is sort of like complacency. You're satisfied with the moment, but you're not necessarily happy. You feel comfortable, and you're not angry. Content is when we keep our mouths flat. You might have one side raised, not in a smile, just sort of half expression.

And lastly, happiness—This is undoubtedly one of the easiest microexpressions we can pick up on. A smiling person is going to be a happy person. The bigger the smile, the easier it is to understand how they might be feeling. Let's take a more in-depth look into what smiling can tell us about another person.

The Influence of Smiles

Fake smiling is frequent because it's a way to make the other person know that we're okay with what's going on, but we might not necessarily feel that emotion.

You can tell somebody is fake smiling by their eyes. Somebody who is fake smiling will not have any wrinkles around their eyes, and their eyebrows will be completely normal. Somebody who is genuinely smiling will have slightly raised eyebrows and lines in the corners of their eyes.

While their mouth might look the same, it's the top of their face that you can use to determine whether somebody's smile is genuine or not.

Some studies show that smiling can make you look younger, thinner, and generally like a more exciting person. Those who smile more might live longer. More research needs to be conducted to determine if this is the truth or just a coincidence. However, some research has helped us realize that people tend to have longer lifespans based on how frequently they smile.

When somebody is smiling, and their mouth is slightly open, then you know that they're thrilled. However, if they're smiling and their mouth is free, and they are genuinely using their eyes, it could be a sign of fear or anxiety. They might be feeling uncomfortable, but they're using a smile to try to suit the situation. What we have to understand about smiles more than anything else is that the other person might not be that happy, but they're at least letting us know that they're feeling generally good. A smile can be a potent tool. Practice smiling in the mirror to make it look more genuine. Fake smiling isn't advantageous in your personal relationships. However, a genuine smile can help in a business and professional setting; it makes everybody feel better, more relaxed, calmer, and more collected (Selig, 2016).

Head Movements
Your head is one of the most critical parts of your body. It houses the brain, after all. Simultaneously, our head movements can tell us a ton about how we might be feeling. Notice the way somebody uses their head when they're talking to you.

A head turned downwards can be a way of protecting your neck and your chin from getting hurt. It can be a subconscious way of protecting the jugular to ensure that no outside threat could kill you. This is done sometimes when we might be angry, sad, or fearful in general as a way of trying to protect ourselves. If their head is down and they're looking up at you, then they might simply just be tired and want to rest. If their head is down and they are looking from left to right, it can be a sign of fear. If their head is down and looking down, it might be a sign of sadness or depression.

Notice the way that they turn their heads too. Our leaders can tell us a lot about what is most interesting to us, though we might often turn our entire bodies towards the thing that is causing intrigue.

Often, people simply turn their heads towards things that they are more interested in. It can be a way for us to rotate our ears to hear better and direct our focus towards something that's making us intrigued.

Somebody tilting their head from side to side might also be showing you that they are interested in what you are talking about. They can also be trying to make you feel more comfortable and using it as a way to be a little bit more flirtatious. Nodding or shaking is another powerful way we use our heads. Those who bow in approval will frequently be in agreement with what you're saying.

Disapproval is shaking the head from left to right. If somebody is actively saying, "Yes," they agree out loud and still nod their head up and down. It could be a sign of encouragement and that we are still in approval.

But if it's left to right, then it might be a sign of their true feelings that they're trying to hide from you again. Consider cluster movements and notice the head in conjunction with microexpressions. This will give you the most authentic insight into how somebody might be trying to use their body.

Chapter 6:
How to Understand Nonverbal Cues and its Benefits

How the Brain Controls Body Language?

The reason nonverbal language never lies is that it happens unconsciously. We can consciously control the things we say to lie or share half-truths, but the body will still show the truth. Why does this happen?

Humans have evolved to communicate in a nonverbal manner. An ancient system lives inside our brain that understands and conveys intentions or emotions through physical movements. This part of the brain is called the limbic system. It works in a precise manner. The amygdala is the key player in the limbic system and is located in the medial temporal lobe. It works by helping us process emotions.

There is an interesting evolutionary story that explains how the limbic system came to be. It takes us through how water-dwelling creatures became land roaming and evolved into walking, talking, and hunting humans.

Something hard to believe for most is that creatures have evolved from common ancestors. These ancestors lived in the water 360 million years ago. The struggle to survive and climatic changes forced them to move to the land. Their fins turned into limbs to walk, and their skin became tougher to handle the harsh climate.

About 320 to 310 million years ago, the reptile evolved. This was when the limbic system began to develop. The reflexive system of the breed, feed, flight, and the fight began. The part of the brain this created consisted of the cerebellum and brain stem. The behavior of the reptile is predictable, but it is what helped them to survive. Emotions didn't exist until mammals evolved.

When mammals emerged, they had a deliberate social behavior, unlike their reptile ancestors. This could be connected to their habitation, bonding, nurturing, reproduction, and changed metabolism. A mammal's offspring grows inside of them until they reach a certain stage. They are fed by secretions from the mammary glands, and they control their temperature to adjust to different climates.

The new brain structure, called the cortex, for mammals was built upon the reptilian complex. This new brain section consisted of the insula, orbital frontal cortex, cingulate gyrus, hippocampus, and amygdala. Even though mammals were superior in their survival, they naturally used the fight or flight approach, a reptilian act. They invented other ways to work around this approach through planned movements, expressions, and behavior. Emotions were a great gift, as well as being able to smell different things and recall these scents. This helped mammals to endure different circumstances. This caused them to spread across the planet.

Finally, the common ancestor of apes and humans appeared- the primate. It is possible that they evolved from mammals that were more skilled at climbing trees for shelter and food. The primate's brain developed more complex parts to help them adapt to new environments and social challenges. They have better systems to coordinate movements on the ground and in trees. They could plan and think. Their vision also improved, and they could recall scenes.

As the climate changed, parts of these primates remained in wooded areas, leaving in the trees. Others were forced to start roaming the ground when their trees were replaced by brush. These primates began walking on two legs with the hands free to farm, fish, hunt, make tools, and gather food. They started to build and live in fixed shelters.

This ability to walk on two feet changed their movement and behavior patterns and how they communicated. Making different sounds, gestures, and facial expressions helped express their feelings to the others in the group. Through various civilizations, this continued to be a unique part of their lifestyle and communication. This created their cultural and social norms and ethics.

For us modern humans, the neocortex is the most advanced part of the brain. This rests above all of the old brain sections. This section of the brain is why we can solve problems, figure out math problems, navigate our way around, perform introspection, learn other languages, use our imagination, and reason. This is also the area that helps us regulate our emotions, harbor feelings, and control a few of our limbic system's impulses. The limbic brain controls all of our nonverbal communication, and we can't completely control it with our neocortex.

Emotional and visual memory can cause us to act in ways that our ancestors would. We feel comfortable in favorable situations and uncomfortable when in danger or distress. When we are placed in a threatening situation, we tend to act like other mammals or reptiles.

Non Verbal Signals

Being able to communicate well is an important part of succeeding in the professional and personal world, but it is not the words you say that scream. Rather, it is your body language. Your eye contact, tone of voice, posture, gestures, and facial expressions are your best communication tools. They can undermine, confuse, offend, draw others in, build trust, or put people at ease.

There are many times where what a person says and what their body language says is completely different. Nonverbal communication can do five things:

- Accent – It can underline or accent your verbal message.
- Complement – It can complement or add to what you are verbally saying.
- Substitute – It can be used in place of a verbal message.
- Contradict – It can go against what you are verbally trying to say, making your listener think you are lying.
- Repeat – It can strengthen and repeat your verbal message.

Here are several different forms of nonverbal communication:

- Facial expressions – The face is expressive and can express several emotions without saying one word. Unlike the things we say and other forms of body language, facial expressions are often very universal.

- Posture and body movement – Take a moment to think about how you view people based on how they hold up their head, walk around, stand, and sit. The way a person carries provides a lot of information.
- Gestures – These are woven into our life. You speak animatedly; argue with your hands, beckon, point, and wave. However, gestures vary across cultures.
- Eye contact – Since sight tends to be the strongest sense for most people, it is an important part of nonverbal communication. The way a person looks at, you can tell you whether they are attracted to you, hostile, affectionate, or interested. It also helps the conversation flow.

Nonverbal communication can go wrong in many different ways. It is quite easy to confuse different signals.

The Lower Body

The arms can share a lot of information. The hands can share more, but the legs provide us with the exclamation point and tell users exactly what a person is thinking. The legs can tell you if a person is comfortable and open. They can also show dominance or show where they want to go.

Shy Tangle
This tends to be something that women do more often than men, but anybody who starts to feel timid or shy will sometimes entangle their legs crossing them under and over to try blocking out bad emotions and make themselves look small. There is another shy leg twirl that people can do while standing. This movement's actual act is crossing one leg over the other and hooking that foot behind the knee as if they are trying to scratch an itch.

Smarty Pants
This is a very apparent position where a person tries to make themselves look bigger. They are typically seated with the legs splayed open and leaned back. They may even spread their arms out and lock them behind their head. This is often used by those who are feeling confident, superior, or dominant.

Touching

A person, when standing, can only touch their thighs or bottom. They can seductively do this, or they can slap their legs as if saying, "Let's go." It can also indicate irritation. This is where paying attention to the context of the conversation is important.

The Upper Body

The upper body language will often show signs of defensive signs because the arms can easily be used as a shield. But upper-body language also involves the chest. Here are some languages of the upper body:

The Superman

This is a common move by models, bodybuilders and was made popular by Superman. This can have many different meanings depending on how a person uses it. In the animal world, animals try to make themself look bigger when they feel threatened. If you watch a house cat, when they get spooked, they stretch their legs, and their fur stands on end. Humans also have this, even though it isn't as noticeable. This is why we get goosebumps. Since we can't make ourselves look bigger anymore, we have come up with arm gestures like placing our hands on our waist. This indicates that a person is getting ready to act assertively.

This is common in athletes before a game or a wife nagging at her spouse. A guy who is flirting with a girl will use this to appear assertive. This is what is referred to as a readiness gesture.

Chest Thrust Outward

If a person pushes their chest out, they are trying to draw attention to that part of them, and it can also be used as a type of romantic display. Women understand that some men are programmed to become aroused by breasts. When you notice a woman pushing her chest out, she may be inviting intimate relations. Men thrust their chest out to show off their chest and possibly to hide their gut. The difference is men do this to women and other men.

Profiled Chest

If a person is standing sideways or angled at 45 degrees, they are trying to accentuate the thrust-out chest. Women may do this to show off the curve of their breasts, and men to show off their profile.

Leaning

If a person leans forward, it moves them closer to the other person. There are two meanings to this. First, it tells you that they are interested in something, which could just be what you are saying. But, this movement can also show romantic interest.

Second, a lean-forward can invade personal space, hence announcing a threat. This is often an aggressive display. This is an unconscious thing that powerful people do.

The Hands

The human hands have 27 bones, and they are an expressive part of our bodies. This gives us a lot of capability to handle our environment.

Reading palms isn't about looking at the lines on the hands. After a person's face, the hands are the best source for body language.

Hand signals might be small, but they show what our subconscious is thinking. A gesture might be exaggerated and done using both hands to establish a point.

Shaping

The hands can cut our words into the air to emphasize the things we are saying and our meaning. They are trying to create a visualization out of nothing.

If a man is trying to describe the size of the fish he caught on his fishing trip, he might try to show the shape by indicating with his hands. He could also carve out a specific shape that he would like his ideal mate to be. Other gestures might be cruder when they hold certain body parts and move sexually.

Holding

A person with cupped hands is indicating they can gently hold onto something. They show delicacy or holding onto something fragile. Hands that are gripping show desire, ownership, or possessiveness. The tighter their fist is, the stronger they are feeling an emotion.

If a person is holding their own hands, they are trying to comfort themselves. They could also be trying to restrain themselves, so they allow someone else to talk. It might be used if they are angry, and it is keeping them from attacking. If they are wringing their hands, they are feeling very nervous.

Holding their hands behind their back shows they are confident by opening up their front. They might conceal their hands to hide their tension. If one hand is holding onto the other arm, the tighter and higher the grip, the more they are tense.

Two hands could show different desires. If one is forming a fist with the other holding it back, it might be showing that they want to punch someone.

A person who is lying tries to control their hands. If they hold them still, you might want to get suspicious. Remember that these are only indicators, and you need to look for other signals.

If a person looks like they are holding an object like a cup or pen, this shows they are trying to comfort themselves. If a person is holding a cup, but they are holding it close where it looks like they are "hugging" the cup, they are hugging themselves. Holding onto an item using both hands makes a closed position.

Items could be used as a distraction to release nervous energy, like holding a pen but doodling, clicking it off and on or fiddling with it.

If their hands are clenched together in front of them but relaxed, with their thumbs at rest, this could show pleasure.

Greeting

Our hands are used to greet others. The most common is the hand-shake. Opening of the palm shows they don't have any concealed weapons. This is used when waving, saluting, and greetings.

This is when we get to touch another person, and it could send many different signals.

Dominance is indicated by shaking hands and placing another one on top. How strong and how long they shake your hands tells you that they are deciding when to stop the handshake.

Affection can be shown with the duration and speed of the hand-shake, smile, or touching with the other hand. The similarity be-tween this one and the dominant can lead to situations when a dom-inant person tries to pretend they are friendly.

Submission is shown by a palm up, a floppy handshake that is some-times clammy and comes with fast withdrawal.

Many handshakes will use vertical palms that show equality. They will be firm but not crushing and for an exact amount of time, so both parties know when they need to let go.

Waving is an easy way to greet somebody and can easily be per-formed from afar.

Salutes are usually only done by the military, where the style is pre-scribed.

Control

If they are holding their hands with the palms facing downward, they might be figuratively restraining or holding onto someone else. This might be an authoritative action telling you to stop now, or it might be a request asking you to calm down. This will appear with the dominant hand placed on top of a handshake. If they are leaning on their desk with their palms down, it usually shows dominance.

If their palms are facing outward toward another person, they might be trying to push them away or trying to fend them off. They could be saying, "stop, don't come closer."

If they are pointing their finger or whole hand, they might be telling a person to leave now.

The Face

A person's facial expressions can help us figure out if we believe or trust what they are saying. The most trustworthy expression will have a slight smile and a raised eyebrow. This expression shows confidence and friendliness.

We often make judgments about how intelligent someone is by their facial expressions. People who have a narrow face and a prominent nose were thought to be very intelligent. People who smile and have joyous expressions can be judged as being intelligent rather than a person who looks angry.

Eyes

Many people refer to the eyes as the "windows to the soul" because they can reveal a lot about what we are thinking and feeling.

Size of Pupils

This can be a very subtle signal. You might have heard the expression "bedroom eyes." If a person's eyes are very dilated, they could be aroused or very interested.

Blinking

This is a natural bodily function, but you need to pay attention to whether or not a person blinks too little or too much. People that blink rapidly might indicate they are feeling uncomfortable or distressed. When a person doesn't blink enough, they may be trying to control how their eyes move. Someone playing poker might blink less because they are trying to look unexcited about the hand they were dealt with.

Eye Gaze

When a person looks at you as you two are talking, they are paying attention and showing interest. Prolonged eye contact might feel threatening. If you break eye contact and look away quickly, it could indicate that you are trying to hide your real feelings, are uncomfortable, or are distracted.

Mouth

Mouth movements and expressions are needed when trying to read body language. Chewing on the lower lip might indicate a person is feeling insecure, fearful, or worried.

When coughing or yawning, if they cover their mouth, it might indicate they are trying to be polite.

Chapter 7:
Can You Detect a Lie Through Body Language?

A lie can be defined as an assertion that is believed to be forced to simply deceive somebody. Lies involve a variety of interpersonal and psychological functions for the people who use them. People use lies for various reasons which are, at most times, best known to them only. It is believed that every human being can lie. Multiple research has suggested that on an average day, people tell one or two lies a day. Some surveys have shown that 96 percent of people admitted to telling a lie at times, while 60 percent of a research study done in the United States claimed that they do not lie at all. However, the researchers found at least half of that number were lying. Scientists say that there are ways to easily spot a lie or know when you are being lied to. Lies can be intended to protect someone while others are very serious, like covering up a crime. People do not know what ways they can use to detect a lie, and most of them tell themselves that they can easily detect a lie. You can easily recognize a lie by noting the nonverbal cues that people use. For example, a liar cannot look you directly in the eye; however, researchers have proven that this might not necessarily work. In 2006, Bond and De Pablo found out that only 54 percent of people could detect a lie in a laboratory setting. Investigators also do not find it easy to detect a lie and can easily be fooled into believing what is not true. Most people believe that trusting your instincts always is the best way to avoid being fooled.

Gesture
This is a form of nonverbal communication where body actions tend to speak or communicate particular messages. Gestures include the movement of hands, feet, face, and other body parts. Gestures enable one to communicate nonverbally to express a variety of feelings and thoughts. For example, people can communicate none verbally when they are in trouble and need somebody's help. The gesturing process comes from the brain, which is used by speech and sign language. It is believed that language came from manual gestures that were being used by the Homo sapiens. This theory is known as the gestural theory brought about by the renowned philosopher Abbe de Condillac in the 18th century. However, the use of gestures can be a way to note when somebody is lying to you. Some people find it hard

to control their body motions when telling a lie. That is why gestures are used to detect when somebody is lying to you. Different body expressions will tell you when a person is lying.

The Mouth Cover

This gesture has been at most times used in childhood. A person lying to you will cover their mouth when trying to prevent themselves from saying the deceitful words. Most people do not entirely cover their mouths but use just a few fingers covering the lips. Other people may try to fake a cough to get a chance to cover their mouths, which by the way, does not make any difference whether they cover it fully or partly. However, this gesture needs to be carefully examined before concluding that the person is lying. If the person covering the mouth is the one talking, it is most likely that they are lying. If the one covering the mouth is the one listening, then this might show that they are carefully listening to what is being said and might be probably thinking that you are not sincere with them. People who can note this behavior cannot be easily fooled, manipulated, or controlled in any way. The liar will always be afraid of approaching the person since they are afraid their intentions will easily be noticed. This reduces the rate at which people use others to their advantage, thereby influencing the community ethically.

The Nose Touch

Most people that lie tend to always touch their noses while talking. After letting go of their mouth, they tend to touch their nose and fake that they are itching. It is almost instant to note when it is just a normal nose itch or when someone is trying to use it to hide a lie. A normal itch can be relieved quickly by just a simple scratch, but if someone keeps scratching and touching their noses, it most probably means they are lying.

The Eye Rub

The brain tends to use the eye trick as a way of hiding deceit. People who lie tend to rub their eyes to hide the clear tell in their eyes that indicates they are lying. Many people find it difficult to maintain eye contact when they are lying, and they tend to shy off every time they look at the person they are lying to. People say that the eyes tend to create a sign of doubt to the person you are talking to. Most people rub their eyes to hide this sign. It is said that men do it very vigorously while women do it gently without having to hurt themselves much. Being able to recognize this gesture will help the community and society at large to fight off liars.

The Ear Grab
When a person is lying, they tend to touch and play around with their ear lobe as they talk. This makes one feel a bit more comfortable while telling a lie and also trying to block themselves from hearing the words that they are saying. Children tend to cover their eyes when they hear something they suspect is a lie and do not want to hear it.

Scratching the Neck and Other Body Parts
Adults who lie tend to use their index finger for scratching their neck just below their ear lobe. This is done a few times, showing that the person is lying. A person who is lying tends to also put a finger in the mouth when they feel they are under a lot of pressure. Lying creates a very uncomfortable state for people, and they, therefore, are unable to control their feeling of nervousness around the people they are lying to, hence the scratching.

Change in Breathing and the Collar Pull
This gesture was first discovered by Desmond Morris when he noticed that there is always a tingling sensation in the facial and neck tissues, which causes one to rub or scratch a couple of times. The increased blood pressure brings about the sweating of the palms and, at times, even under the armpits. This makes you short of breath when you start suspecting that the person you are deceiving might not be believing you. This is called a reflex action.

The Position Change of the Head
People tend to make quick and sudden head movements after being given a direct question or query. They are likely to be lying about something. They will either retract the head, or be turned face downwards or even be tilted to one side before answering the question you asked them.

Feet Shuffling, Holding a Stare and Standing Still

People who are not moving at all when you engage in a conversation with them should be a call for concern. It is normal that when you two people converse, there is the body's movement in a relaxed way, but if the other person is very rigid and seems relaxed in a very extraordinary way, this could show that probably there is something very off about that person. The shuffling of the feet is brought about by being nervous and uncomfortable. It could also show that the person eagerly wants to leave the conversation as soon as possible. Looking at a person's feet and their movements tell you a lot about what that person is saying. It is renowned that most people cannot maintain eye contact when lying; however, some other people don't move an eye or blink when they are lying to you in a quest to completely get away with their lie and manipulation. Liars tend to use a cold stare when trying to intimidate and control you.

The above-explained gestures are seen in a lot of people who try to manipulate people or lie to them to get what they want. So, it is good to have these skills to help you identify people that play around with your mind or may want to use you to their advantage. Most people who lie will lack words to say since all their tactics have been revealed and learned by everyone.

Facial Expressions

The facial expressions that a person makes tell you a lot, whether they are lying or not. Lies to you become apparent when you can learn these different cues in a conversation. All that goes around someone's face shows either dishonesty or honesty in a conversation. The following are the facial expressions that may tell you that a person is lying:

The Eyes

The eyes are what most people use to note whether the other person is telling the truth or not. The eyes create a link to both imagination and memory. Imagination is often seen as a good thing when one is creating a lie. This is because one can imagine situations in their head and try to figure out the person's reaction after hearing the lie. It is said that when a person looks up and to the left after being asked a question, they are usually trying to recall some information from their memory. Whatever is said by this is believed to be the truth. When someone looks up and to the right, they are utilizing their imagination or, in other words, fabricating information to give to you. This is taken as a lie. However, this might be a little bit confusing for those people that are left-handed. Left-handed people tend to do the opposite of this theory. They look up and to the right when trying to create a lie and look up and to the left when trying to remember some events that took part in the past. The left side of a left-handed person is considered true, while the right side is considered to be a lie. After asking a question, pay close attention to the person's eyes and the direction they move. The eyebrows also tend to raise when they tell the truth and tend to blink or close their eyes a lot to steal time for them to rethink their lie and make sure that their story is kept intact without having to betray themselves through the eyes. Most people that lie also tend to avoid eye contact with the person they are talking to. When forced to make eye contact, they often feel uncomfortable and may even fall short of words, making the other person know that they were trying to lie to them.

Blushing
When a person is telling a lie, they tend to often blush. They become nervous, thereby creating an increase in the body temperature, especially around the face area. Blood tends to flow in the cheeks, causing the liar to blush or shy away. Although blushing can be stimulated by many other things, it is almost inevitable for a liar to blush. This might be a good way also to know when somebody is blushing.

Smiling
A person who lies while smiling does not have a lot of facial expressions like the flickering of the eyes to show that their smile is real. However, liars smile with "dead eyes" that do not brighten up their faces. A real smile has a great effect on the eyes and tends to cause the eyes to either become big or small. This is because more muscles

are used in becoming happy rather than forced demands. A liar always has a fake smile whereby the truth of their lie is revealed by their eyes yet again. Distinguishing between a real and fake smile will help you distinguish between a person telling the truth and one who is lying.

Microexpressions
Facial expressions that easily come and go quickly serve as the best indicators that a person might be lying. These expressions are known as micro-expressions. These expressions prove to be great lie detectors and reveal the raw truth. These expressions also reveal if there is something wrong since it is hard to hide these expressions. However, it is good to note that not all microexpressions reveal that a person is lying, so it is highly advised that you be trained on how best to note and differentiate these feelings. Before concluding that the person you are questioning is lying, it is advisable that you first check on the circumstance and situation at hand.

Speech
The way a person speaks while in front of you can tell a lot about truths and lies. Liars tend to repeat themselves a lot while speaking because they are not sure of what they are saying and are struggling to convince themselves of their lies. A person lying to you tends to speak quickly, enabling them to bring out the lies in a very fast and consistent way. They are often left wondering whether the lie they told would be believable, causing them to have an increase in heartbeats. Liars tend to add more or extra details to their stories to convince their listeners that what they are saying is true. They take brief moments to rehearse or go over the answers they had rehearsed before to ensure that they do not make any mistakes to make their listeners doubt them. At times, they become defensive about their answers and tend to play the victim if they think their lie is not going as planned. However, the liar does not stand a chance if the person hearing the lies has expertise in understanding and knowing when a person is lying to them or creating a lie.

Voice Change

Gregg McCrary, a retired federal bureau of investigations criminal profiler, stated that a person's voice might change abruptly when they tell a lie. This strategy works by first noting their speech patterns by asking simple questions, for example, where they live. By this, one can monitor the various changes in the speaking tones when faced with a more challenging question. A person who learns this art can easily tell when a person is telling or trying to formulate a lie.

These facial expressions clearly show that people must learn these arts to deal with people in the society who love manipulating others. These people tend to confuse people by lying to them and making these lies true so that they can get away with their lies. A person who is not able to identify such kinds of people is at a higher risk of getting blackmailed by these people and making you do what they want to do, for example, commit a crime for them.

Chapter 8:
How Body Language Improves Your Mindset

Our body language is the way we speak with the outside world—and the more significant part of us don't realize we are doing it! Body language phenomenally affects the center of who you are as an individual. It impacts our posture and physiological well-being, yet it can likewise change our psychological viewpoint, an impression of the world, and others' perception of us.

How Our Body Imparts

We utilize our body language to communicate our musings, thoughts, and feelings; we synchronize body developments to the words we express. We impart purposefully through activities like shrugging our shoulders or applauding just as through inadvertent correspondence like twisting in on ourselves or guiding our feet an alternate way toward the individual we talked about. Before spoken language was made, our body language was the primary technique for correspondence. Our body is our major method to interact with life!

How Can It Influence Our State of Mind?

Our body language is how we communicate with our outside world, likewise how we associate with ourselves. How would you treat yourself? Do you slouch over when you walk, or do you walk tall and proud? It is true to say that you are thankful for each development that your body makes for you?

Most likely than not, we regularly underestimate our body; we frequently decide to condemn it. Body language can impact our physical body and posture. However, it can likewise change how we are feeling. Having a great attitude can affect misery and cause us to keep up more elevated levels of confidence and energy when confronted with pressure.

An up and coming field of psychology, known as installed comprehension, asserts that the association between our body and our general surroundings doesn't merely impact us. However, we are personally woven into the way that we think.

Four Different Ways You Can Change Your Body Language

The followings are four ways you can change your body language.

Flip Around That Glare!

Grinning and snickering is infectious! A complete report on smiling found that a grin that draws in the mouth and moves the skin around the eyes can enact the cerebrum examples of positive feelings. So, grin and grin frequently! Regardless of whether you are having an awful day, grin at any rate! It may very well assist you with turning the day around!

Collapsing Your Arms

We regularly do it when we feel shaky, anxious, or disturbed. The physical obstruction gives others the feeling that we are cut off and detached from them.

The intersection of the arms is a broad idea to be an antagonistic body posture anyway. A few investigations have indicated that crossing the arms can cause individuals to progressively industrious when they feel like stopping.

If you believe you need a little additional lift to take a stab at making some regular mindset boosting homegrown cures like Hyperiforce. It contains concentrates of the bloom hypericum frequently utilized as a treatment for low mind-set and gentle nervousness.

Force Presenting

One of the significant specialists in the zone of body language is Amy Cuddy. She made members remain in high force stances and low force models for two minutes before sending them into a top weight talk with the condition. She estimated levels of the pressure hormone cortisol and the predominance hormone testosterone. The outcomes demonstrated that those remaining in high force present had expanded testosterone degrees and lower cortisol levels than those in little force present.

Quit Slumping

It may appear glaringly evident; however, slumping not just influences your spine. It can change your state of mind! Indeed, slumping can prompt back agony and an irregular spine arrangement. Intellectually, it can leave you feeling miserable, lacking vitality, and shut off from others. Sitting and standing up straighter can help settle back torment and just as enrich your life and lift your state of mind.

Changing your posture can be trying for your body from the outset, particularly on the off chance you are accustomed to slumping over for significant periods! You may feel muscle hurts in the neck, back, and bears—don't stress, this will pass! Meanwhile, I'd suggest utilizing Atrogel, a natural relief from discomfort cure containing new concentrates of arnica blossoms.

Improve Your Posture to Improve Your Temperament!

Body language likely isn't the first thing that comes to mind experiencing a low state of mind. However, investigating our body language can reveal to us how we are truly feeling. Our body language has an immediate connection to our temperament, similarly that our mindset influences our posture.

Simple ways you can fix your posture to adjust your state of mind are:

- Smile when you are having a terrible day!
- Unfold your arms when you feel anxious and permit yourself to be available to circumstances.
- Turning the palms of your hands forward when you walk will urge the shoulders to unwind back as opposed to moving advances.
- Power present before pressure instigating situations like prospective employee meet-ups.

Body Language Signs When Someone Hides Something from You

Untrustworthiness. It happens in many connections—and a great deal of the time, it accomplishes more mischief than anything. It's once in a while ever astute to keep insider facts from your partner in a relationship. You never need to keep your partner in obscurity about a lot of things in your lives together. That is simply out and out insolent. It shows that you don't regard them enough to recognize that they are deserving of reality. You are saying that they aren't sufficient to be determined what's genuine—and that is, in every case, terrible in a relationship. You generally need to confess all to your partner, particularly about vital issues encompassing your relationship.

Be that as it may, a considerable number of us are childish. Here and there, reality can be difficult to stomach. Now and then, a fact can place us in an extreme condition of a burden once it's uncovered. So, a great deal of us will turn to lie just to spare our butts. Your man may be blameworthy of doing as such. He may be keeping you out of the loop about something that he ought to be opening up to you.

What's more, that is hazardous for a relationship. You can't hope to make your link work if you're not being taken care of the entirety of the best possible realities. You generally need to ensure that you know all that is going on to don't wind up getting tricked or bushwhacked by anything.

Men aren't generally the best verbal communicators. You may likely know this at this point. Be that as it may, he consistently communicates through his body language and physical developments. His intuition may be disclosed to you many things about himself without seeing it in any event. You simply need to willingly volunteer to ensure that you spot out the signs when they present themselves. You need to ensure that you keep steady over things in your relationship.

Getting and Understanding Nonverbal Signals

Lauren murmured. She'd quite recently gotten an email from her chief, Gus, saying that the item proposition she'd been taking a shot at would not have been closed down. It didn't bode well. Seven days prior, she'd been in a gathering with Gus, and he'd appeared to be extremely positive about everything. Of course, he hadn't looked, and he continued watching out of the window at something. In any case, she'd recently put that down to him being occupied. Furthermore, he'd said that "the task will most likely stretch the go-beyond."

On the off chance that Lauren had discovered somewhat progressively about body language, she'd have understood that Gus was attempting to reveal to her that he wasn't "sold" on her thought. He simply wasn't utilizing words.

The Most Effective Method to Read Negative Body Language

Monitoring negative body language in others can permit you to get on implicit issues or awful emotions. Along these lines, in this area, we'll feature some negative nonverbal signs that you should pay individual minds to.

Troublesome Conversations and Defensiveness

Troublesome or tense discussions are an awkward unavoidable truth grinding away. Maybe you've needed to manage an annoying client or expected to converse with somebody about their terrible attitude. Or then again, perhaps you've arranged a significant agreement.

In a perfect world, these circumstances would be settled in tranquility. Be that as it may, regularly, they are entangled by sentiments of apprehension, stress, preventiveness, or even resentment. However, we may also attempt to shroud them; these feelings regularly appear in our body language. For instance, on the chance that somebody is showing at least one of the accompanying practices, he will probably be withdrawn, uninvolved, or miserable:

- Arms collapsed before the body.
- Insignificant or tense outward appearance.
- The body got some distance from you.

- Eyes depressed, keeping in touch.
- Keeping away from unengaged audiences

At the point when you have to convey an introduction or to work together in a gathering, you need the individuals around you to be 100 percent locked in. Here are some "obvious" signs that individuals might be exhausted or uninterested in what you're stating:

- Sitting drooped, with heads sad.
- Looking at something different, or into space.
- Squirming, picking at garments, or tinkering with pens and telephones.
- Composing or doodling.

Step by Step Instructions to Project Positive Body Language

When you utilize positive body language, it can add solidarity to the verbal messages or thoughts you need to pass on and help you abstain from imparting blended or befuddling signs. In this segment, some fundamental postures you can embrace to extend fearlessness and receptiveness will be portrayed.

Establishing a Confident First Connection

These tips can assist you in adjusting your body language, so you establish an extraordinary first connection:

- Have an open posture. Be loose; however, don't slump! Sit or stand upstanding and place your hands by your sides. Abstain from remaining with your hands on your hips; it will cause you to seem more significant, conveying animosity or craving to rule.
- Utilize a firm handshake. However, don't become overly energetic! You don't need it to get unbalanced, more regrettable, or excruciating for the other individual. On the chance that it does, you'll likely seem to be impolite or forceful.
- Keep in touch. Try to maintain eye contact with the other person for a couple of moments, one after another. It will give the impression that you're right and locked in. Abstain from transforming it into a gazing match!

162

- Abstain from touching your face. There's a typical discernment that individuals who contact their appearances while addressing questions are being untrustworthy. While this isn't in every case valid, it's ideal to abstain from twirling your hair or touching and/or scratching your mouth or nose, especially if your point is to seem to be reliable.

Chapter 9:
The Five C's of Nonverbal Communication

For the early human ancestors, decisions made instantaneously based on subtle visual clues may mean life or death. First impressions today still bring about automatic responses, but these may or may not be accurate.

When you see someone with arms crossed, do you think they are just feeling defensive and using their arms as a barrier? Or is it an act of superiority and dominance? Or maybe it's just a comfortable position for them?

Nonverbal signals help you form these quick impressions, and this is a basic survival instinct. But although this innate ability may come naturally and automatically, not all first impressions are correct and accurate.

The human brain is hardwired to respond automatically to particular nonverbal cues, resulting from millions of years of evolution. But our ancestors were exposed to challenges and threats that were much different from what we go through every day.

These automatic responses should be filtered and analyzed because we now live in a society wherein nuances and restrictions add layers to what could have been simple personal interactions. For example, a workplace setting with corporate culture and policies add to interaction complexities bringing about a different set of guidelines and restrictions for behavior.

In her book, 'The Nonverbal Advantage: Secrets and Science of Body Language at Work," author Carol Kinsey Goman formulated five filters that you can use to sift through first impressions. These are culture, consistency, congruence, clusters, and context and are collectively called the five C's of nonverbal communication.

Culture
Cultural heritage influences nonverbal communication. When reading nonverbal cues, the amount of stress that the person is under should be considered. A high emotional level brings up gestures that are specific to certain cultures.

Understanding cultural differences can help you read body language more accurately. Let's take the simple gestures for 'yes' and 'no,' for example. When you agree to something, you move your head up and down; otherwise, you do it from side to side. This is a common set of gestures for many cultures. The Eskimos, however, do it the other way. And what a big misunderstanding it could have been if you read the gesture the wrong way.

Another obvious cultural difference is proximity when talking with another person. People stand closer to each other when talking in Western countries, and this is an accepted norm in their culture, showing more intimacy and closeness. However, those in the middle east respect other people's personal space and tend to leave a bigger space in between.

Cultures may not differ only between countries but in different regions of the same country as well. Let's take Japan, for example. In Tokyo, the nation's capital, it's common to see people half-running around as they try to reach the train or bus on time on their way to work. This contrasts the leisurely gait of people from the provinces of Japan.

Another factor that may change a person's body language is his or her profession. A person standing or sitting down with back straight may be seen as someone brimming with confidence, while someone with slouched shoulders and hunched back as an introvert. Someone trained in ballet dancing or with the military will have a proper upright posture, while those who spend their days in office work might always slouch. But their postures may not define their personality nor their nonverbal communication cues.

Understanding the culture you are currently in while trying to interpret body language is critical as this can significantly modify the signals.

Consistency

The baseline of a person's behavior is when they are in a relaxed or stress-free condition. Understanding this baseline is important when comparing it with gestures brought about by stress or other stimuli.

Look at a person. How does he normally stand or sit when relaxed? How does he normally look around? When discussing a non-threatening topic, how does he respond? This behavioral baseline can help you recognize significant changes in a person's gestures in different situations.

A teacher might have a student in the class holding up his head with the palm of his hand and quickly interpret it as boredom. But if the teacher looks for consistency, a pattern might show up that nullifies this first impression. So instead of blaming himself for the quality of his lecture, he can talk to the student about what makes him tired coming to the class.

You need to examine whether the behavior being shown by the other person is atypical. If he's known to be someone who is habitually unflappable, warning signs should carry even more weight. Knowing that person's baseline behavior is very helpful before you try to interpret his expressions.

Congruence

When a person speaks, and you can feel that the words, tone of voice, and body language are all telling the same thing, there's a good chance that you are getting a true signal. But when that person tells one thing, but the nonverbal signals don't show a similar pattern, you should be alerted that they're trying to deceive you.

This is called testing for congruence. When a person's thoughts and words are aligned, which means they believe what they say, you'll see that their body language corroborates what is being said.

If you see telltale signs of incongruence, you may be able to conclude that the other person is not telling the truth. A person agreeing with what you said while moving his head from side to side or saying they're happy with slouched shoulders and head bowed down are examples of incongruence.

Supposed you had an argument with your partner and when you approached her after an hour to ask if she's still mad at you, she answered, 'NO!' with a stern voice and crossed arms, what do you think the real answer is? You can be pretty sure that she meant otherwise because her verbal answer is not congruent with her body language.

Incongruence may not be a sign of an intentional lie, and the person may just be undergoing inner conflict on what they're saying versus while they are thinking about the subject.

Congruence between body and verbal languages helps create stronger trust between two parties. It may be from one person to another or an audience. When your verbal cues are aligned with your body language, you are perceived as being authentic, and people will see that you are someone worthy of their trust.

Clusters

During a conversation, you might see dozens of different nonverbal signals from the other person. In situations like this, you should not be putting significant meaning on any single action. You should instead be looking for clusters.

A gesture cluster is a group of actions, postures, and movements that indicate a common point. A single gesture such as crossing arms can be interpreted with different meanings, or it may not have any meaning at all. But when combined with other nonverbal signals like a stern look, a headshake, or a scowl, the meaning becomes clearer.

That is why you should always be looking for behavioral clusters. When viewed independently, a single gesture might have a different meaning when combined with other nonverbal signals.

A sad face may or may not indicate anxiety, but the symptoms begin to become clearer if you see other indications. Other signs may include foot movement, shifting of weight, heavy swallowing, rapid blinking, heavy perspiration, and rubbing of palms seen from the other person indicates an anxiety attack—something hard to conclude if you only focus on a single action.

Effective leadership, for example, requires you to level with your team members. During a staff meeting, you may take off your jacket and sit at the center instead of the head of the table, which might indicate informality to make others around you feel more relaxed. But it can be further emphasized by leaning forward when someone speaks, making eye contact, and showing interest in the subject. This is an effective way to conduct a meeting where there is an open exchange of questions and ideas without considering position or rank.

Context

Context is about considering everything going on around the non-verbal cues such as location, what previously transpired, anything else going on, and other factors that may affect the body language. The meaning behind nonverbal communication can significantly change when the context also changes.

Let's take crossing arms as an example. When a person is being scolded and crosses his arms, that can mean that he's being defensive and is preparing a reply. But when the interrogator is the one crossing his arms, it can mean a show of superiority or authority.

The location also has a significant effect on the meaning behind body language. A person shivering slightly and hunching over while waiting at the bus station might be thinking, 'It's cold out here!'. While another person doing the same actions but sitting alone inside a comfortable office might be thinking, 'I need help!'

When you think of a man flailing his arms and screaming loud, you might immediately interpret it as a reaction to danger. But when another man is performing the same action during a football game, your perception of his behavior changes.

When you are having an informal talk with a friend, and he touches his nose, that usually means nothing or just an itchy nose. But if that same friend is on a witness stand and has not touched his nose for an hour but did so when asked an intimidating question, that could indicate deception. The context changed your perception of his body language.

The relationship between two people can also significantly affect the context. When you talk with your team member, boss, or customer, you might display different nonverbal signals depending on who you are communicating with. Other factors that you may need to consider are past encounters, time of day, and the conversation setting (public or private).

Chapter 10:
The Art of Seduction Through Body Language

Making A Great First Impression

People can forget what you said. People can forget what you have done. But they will never forget how you made them feel. Think about it for a few seconds, you also form a first impression of the people you meet for the first time, so you should know that. On occasion, and you will have been wrong judging others ahead of time.
To prevent this from happening to you, we invite you to follow the following tips:

Be Punctual
First of all, you must be punctual. Nobody likes waiting past the agreed time set for a meeting, let alone if it is a job interview. Be aware of this and give yourself enough time to arrive on time because, otherwise, you may not have a second chance.
Watch Body Language
Your body language speaks silently about you. Several studies have shown that it is four times more important than the things you can say. Looking at the person's eyes while talking or shaking hands firmly is important to make a good first impression.

Smile
Although the smile has to do with body language, separating it from the previous point is important to remember. You don't need to show your teeth, but there's nothing that creates a better impression than a big smile. Try not to go from the smile to seriousness very quickly; it will seem that you are forcing it. The key is in naturalness.

Relax
The posture is important to show good body language, but don't look like a robot when trying to control it. Sit straight, but don't be so rigid that people notice it is forced. Relax, and don't be nervous. Enjoy the moment.

Be Yourself

Do not pretend to be someone you are not, because you may notice. So be yourself. This may sound like a cliche, but it is the truth. So try not to lie, because if you get caught, you will be marked with the image of a liar.

Be Positive
Your attitude shows in everything you do. Project a positive attitude, even if you receive criticism or are nervous. If you have an interview or have been with that special someone, you should think that if for some reason the situation does not go as you wanted, it will be great learning.

Be Open and Humble
Humility is one of the values that human beings most appreciate. Try not to be arrogant and be open to others. That creates trust and a good rapport. A great ego can create rejection, so if you want to fall fast, show yourself as a humble and respectful person.

Highlight Your Features
We all have something unique to offer. Perhaps you are an expert in a branch of knowledge that generates curiosity in others or have a great sense of humor. If you still don't know what you can offer, you better do a self-knowledge job right now. Now, seducing a girl or a boy is not the same as seducing an interviewer for a job. So you must also take into account the situation of each moment.

Be Empathetic
To get along with others, you must be empathetic. This means that if you look at the situation from the point of view of others, you will be closer to knowing exactly how to act and leave a good impression on that person.

Body Language Clues That Show a Man Is Interested

Many differences between men and women are caused by several reasons, but they all stem from the root cause – the different biological purposes of men and women. A man is a carrier of variability; a woman is a carrier of heredity, a continuer of the genus. In Chinese philosophy, this corresponds to the concept of the two principles of life (male and female), called "yang" and "yin."
Now, it's time to put your innate traits to good use.

Read His Body Language
Body language is an essential part of communication, whether in the professional or the private sector. We tend to forget it: the body sometimes says more than words. Posture, games, or mimicry: in love, understanding the meaning of the gestures of men may be a serious asset. How to decipher the body language of men? What are the seduction techniques of a man? Can we understand the gestures of men? The good news is several aspects of body language are universal. Here are some elements to observe to learn to decode the body communication of the man who interests you:
The eyes, the mirror of the soul – the gaze is an important aspect of the man's body language, like that of the woman. Does he look at you in a sustained way, a reflection of his confidence in himself? Does he rather have the fleeting eyes of shyness? Or does he have the curious and respectful look of the man who cares about you?

Mimicry of the face – observe his mouth and his eyebrows. What kind of smile does he give you? A smile that is candid and seductive, a nervous smile of the nervous man, or a forced smile of the bored man? Does he raise his eyebrows in astonishment, admiration, or skepticism?

Legs and arms – it takes space, and you have to put them somewhere. Is he constantly moving nervously? Does it cross each other, attentive and refined? Does he stretch them out in front of himself or hold them apart, signs of absolute relaxation? Or is his ankle resting on his knee, which can mean either relaxed or up for some competition?

174

The overall posture – expresses the dominant feeling. If it is slouched, he is likely to be deeply relaxed. If he is curled up, he is probably trying to protect himself and lacks self-confidence. He stands tall? Trust your instincts to see if he's tense, impatient, ready to act, or just elegant.

Here are three elements of the body language of the man that could mean that he pinches for you.
The physical proximity – if he gets into your intimate space, that is to say, he approaches you so that the distance is less than the length of an arm, the language of this man's body tells you he is trying to approach you after following your cues. If this proximity is reduced to physical contact, it is all the more clearer.

The imitation of your gestures – if the body language of a man mimics yours, it is a safe bet that he is under your spell. Likewise, if he regularly touches his face, neck, earlobe or runs his hand through his hair when talking – this man likes you but is a bit shy and wants to get things right.

The best guide? Your intuition.
The best way to understand a man's body language is to listen to your intuition. Do you feel that you like him? Or do you have the feeling that he just wants to put you in his bed and that any other woman will do? On the contrary, do you feel it is mutual love at first sight? You are surely right. Trust your instinct, probably the best guide to decoding the body language of the man you are interested in.

Body Language Clues That Show a Woman Is Interested
You'll know she's accepted you are flirting if immediately after applying social pressure, she is laughing, agreeing, saying something witty, or being playful with you. Pay attention to her sub-communications and body language for other signs of interest (playing with hair, licking her lips, touching you, blushes, the body is squared up to yours) too.

Remember, women feel attraction on an emotional level, not a logical one. If there are no emotions, then there is no possibility of creating attraction. This form of emotional escalation works well because attractive women are used to having sexual power over men.

When you show her that she holds no power over you by being freer, firing off flirtatious and witty comments, and taking a lead role in the interaction, it provokes her to flirt back, which unconsciously suggests that you have equal or greater social value.

It shows that you're not overawed by her physical beauty the way that most men are. It clearly illustrates that you are willing to take social risks and be disliked so that you can speak your truth.

Sometimes, especially when you're first beginning your journey into the dating game, it can be difficult to gauge whether or not a woman wants you to escalate the interaction and get physical. However, there are five common signs that she wants you to move forward and escalate the interaction.

Specifically:

1. You've developed a man to woman vibe, and the tension is increasing.

2. She is holding strong eye contact with you.

3. She is talking to you and sharing herself with you, beyond just normal conversation.

4. She is smiling, laughing, flirting back, and responding well to your conversation.

5. Her body language indicates arousal, e.g., her hips are pointed towards you, she's leaning in your direction, she's playing with her hair, licking her lips, and trying to stay close to you.

Chapter 11:
How to Show Dominance Through Body Language

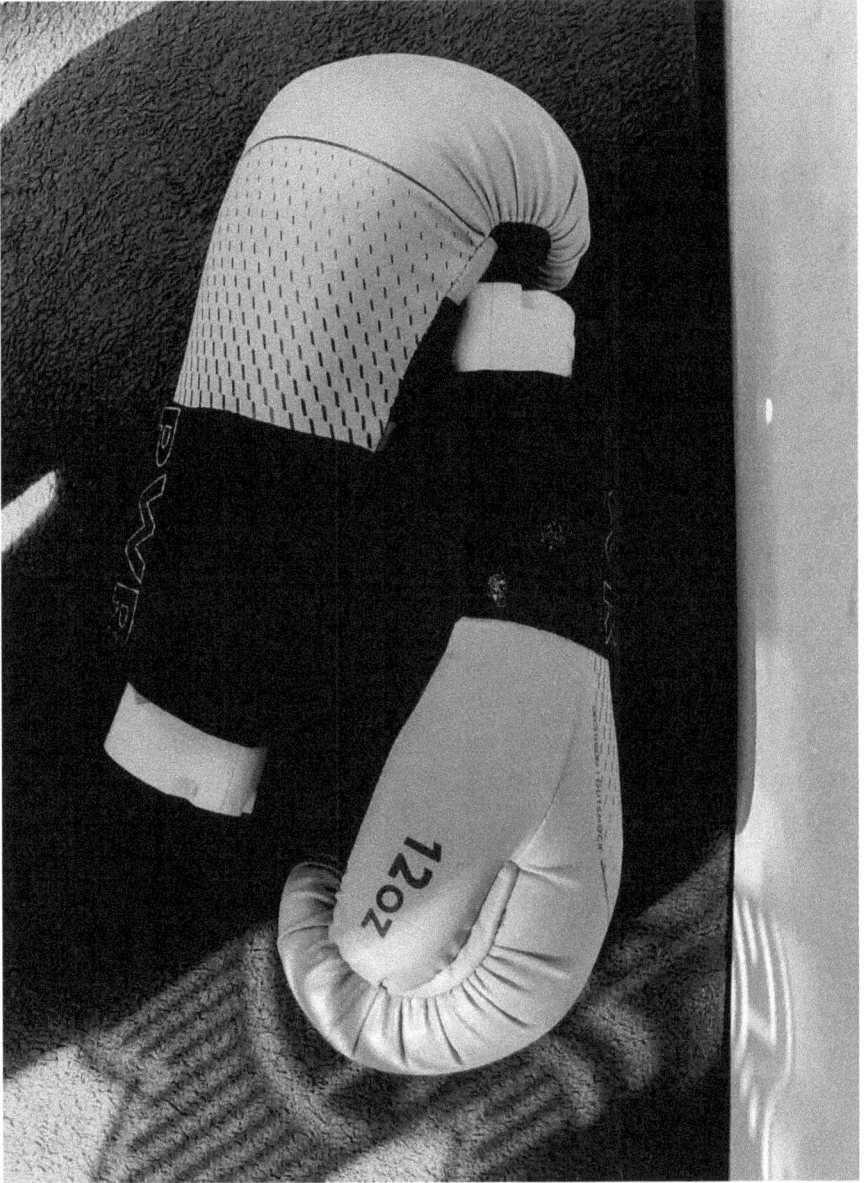

People who want to imply being in charge usually use dominant nonverbal cues. These people may not be aware of these body language signals may not even be aware that they are doing so and may just be a factor in their dominant personality.

Used properly, showing dominance through body language can help you gain respect and popularity, a method usually employed by politicians during the campaign period. Here are some actions that express dominance.

Appearing Larger

Appearing larger and more powerful is an important factor in showing dominance, and this can be traced back to man's prehistoric roots. This action is also evident in animals who fight for dominance. These fights are often settled by size comparison, saving the parties involved from altercations.

This behavioral bias was inherited by modern humans and can be seen practiced when competing with others. Using the same size and body language signal, they try to show their superiority by appearing to be threatening and should be avoided. Here are examples of these size signals:

-       Make your body appear bigger. A bigger person is often seen as more dominant and more threatening. If you have the height advantage, then good for you because you are already large, and this effect comes naturally to you. It's one of the main reasons why taller people tend to be more successful than others, not only in sports but also in the corporate world. Here are some gestures, postures, and body language tricks to appear bigger for the smaller ones.

- Place your hand on your hips. This will make you appear wider than you usually are, thus adding to your size.
- Stand upright. Straightening your back can add inches to your height.
- Sit or stand with your legs apart. This applies to men, and like placing your hands on your hips, it also adds to your 'width.'
- Hold your head and chin up. Another technique you can use to add to your height.

Stand higher. When you are standing higher than the other person, you are in a more dominant position giving you a natural advantage. You can do this by:

- Standing while the other party sits. This instantly gives you the height advantage.
- Standing on a platform or step to give you extra height when compared with the other party
- Standing tall and straight. Tiptoe if you must.
- Wearing a large hat or wear high heel shoes
- Styling your hair to make you look taller. This is common practice with women.

Remember, people who make themselves appear larger or bigger aim to be more dominant, threatening, or powerful.

Claiming Territory

Humans are quite territorial, thanks to our ancestral origins and heritage. People shot a lot of territorial signals, and you can use these to predict behavior. When trying to be more dominant, you can do the following nonverbal signals to claim territory:

- Claim a particular area in a conference room, exhibition center, meeting room, or office room and expect other people to comply with the rules you set for that area.

- Invade the personal space of the other person to imply dominance. You can even emphasize the act with a touch, like lightly holding the arm or patting the person's back, indicating ownership. A study showed that show of affection may not always be why a man touches a woman. Instead, it can be a show of dominance or ownership.

- Invade an area currently owned by the other person. You can sit at the edge of that person's table or on their chair, which is a common gesture of dominance. This move is often used by power-tripping managers or bosses who invade other people's territory to show them who is in charge.

-      Touch or hold the other person's possessions. When this gesture is made with a relaxed composure, it implies that you own what they own, which is another indication of domination. You may pick the other person's favorite pen or phone or rearrange their desk. It's like saying, "what's yours is also mine, and you can't do anything to stop me."

-      Walk in the center of the corridor so that other people stay out of your way. This is a claim to a common territory that implies authority and dominance over others. The same can be observed from some drivers during heavy traffic wherein they don't let other drivers merge into their lane.

-      When the meeting room has a long table, sit at one end. This position is usually reserved for someone with a superior role or power. Sitting here emphasizes your dominance over others.

-      When talking with a group, position yourself at the center, forcing others to pay attention to what you're discussing. Since your back will be vulnerable, ensure that the persons you trust are behind you.

Signaling Superiority
There are various direct or indirect power cues to show if you want to appear dominant, particularly in social contexts. You can either plan these signals or improvise when the need arises. These power signals can be a combination of verbal and nonverbal languages. Here are some of the techniques that you can use:
Show of dominance through wealth

-      Wear expensive clothes, watch, jewelry, accessories, and makeup. Doing so makes you appear rich, powerful, and well-connected.

-      Show off your possessions indirectly. This can be done by paying hefty bills in a relaxed manner, flashing the latest flagship mobile phone, or driving an expensive car.
Show of dominance through control

-        Order a staff or team member to bring you something in front of another person. This implies that you are in charge of the area. For example, you can tell someone to bring you a cup of coffee, print a certain report immediately, or have them call another person and bring that person into the meeting room.

- Controlling and giving orders can also be combined with a display of wealth to emphasize the importance. For example, call your secretary while in the presence of others and have her reserve you a business class flight, a five-star hotel with all the bells and whistles, and a chauffeured luxury car. Showing that you can get whatever you want indicates power and dominance, and this is a move usually exhibited by top corporate executives to impress their customers.

Controlling Time

No, you don't need a time machine for this technique. Similar to dominate other people's space, you can control their time as well by setting a pace for them to follow. You can use nonverbal cues to exert time pressure on other people. Here are some verbal and nonverbal techniques you can use:

Interrupt

-        Interrupt a discussion by leaving early or arriving late

Hurry other people

-        Set a fast pace for other people to follow

-        Walk using wide strides. This implies you're determined a certain goal quickly and that you are confident with your actions. When you're walking with another person, walk a bit faster to set your pace. This shows who's in charge, and the slower person will be forced to also walk fast to keep up.

-        Talk faster than usual. This forces others to also talk fast and give you control of their time.

Slow down other people

-        When talking with another person, interrupt him by asking for a concise and brief talk. This implies you value your time more than his. You can also use this technique when breaking a pace set by another person so you can change the discussion's focus. This may also be effective in counteracting the hurried pace of a dominant person.

Facial Expressions

To show dominance, it's important to extensively use facial expressions to show power and control. Here are some examples.

- Avoid eye contact. To suggest that someone is not important to you, you can simply avoid looking at them.
- Make prolonged eye contact. When you gaze at the other person intensely while proving a point, it implies that you stand by your word and you're not budging an inch. It also shows dominance, being uncooperative and unwilling, and being strong-minded.
- Make a neutral face. This can be very useful during negotiations because making this facial expression can be interpreted by the other person that you are unimpressed. When you hold this facial expression while another person is pitching his product or case enthusiastically, it can cause him to buckle or be unnerved. This is often exhibited during academic debates when a domain or subject expert such as a professor wants to show dominance by showing that he's not interested in others' ideas.
- Smile sparingly. People who want to show dominance smile less often than the submissive ones. Although there's a chance that some people might dislike you, smiling less often shows you mean business and are in control.

Display Your Crotch (Applies Only to Men)

Of course, you need to have your pants on when you do this move or risk spending the night inside the jail. Stand with your feet shoulder-width apart with both feet firmly planted on the ground. This is called standing crotch display and is a very masculine way of highlighting your genitals to show dominance or superiority. You can emphasize this move by 'adjusting' or lightly 'touching' the crotch area. You can also do this technique by sitting down by opening your legs and knees.

It's very uncommon for women to show this gesture because it can be interpreted as an invitation to sexual intimacy. However, some may do so as a show of strength and equality with men.

Counteract Dominance

But what if another person in the room is showing dominance using the techniques mentioned above? You can derail their actions by utilizing these nonverbal strategies:

Return the gaze. If the other person looks you in the eye longer than what you consider normal, look back and return the gaze. You might get distracted by their piercing eyes, but there's a way around that. Instead of looking directly into their eyes, imagine a triangle formed by the eyes and forehead, then look at the center of that triangle.

Initiate the first touch. Just before that person touches you, touch him first. Or retaliate with your touch when he touches you. This shows that you're not one to be messed with or dominated.

Take it slow. When the dominant person is trying to rush you, breathe slowly, remain calm, and slow down the pace. This can imply that there's no need to hurry. Show that the slower pace you're trying to set is more ideal, and be persistent about it. This applies to both walking and talking.

Use humor. A dominant person always aims to take over conversations. Break that dominance by telling a joke and take back control of the conversation. You can get a laugh by telling a joke or using funny nonverbal actions. You can use this break to shift the discussion back to your preferred topic.

Body language can be used to show dominance and influence the action of others. You can also use it to counteract dominance being imposed by others.

Chapter 12:
Using Body Language in Your Daily Life

Now, let's take a closer look into something that you can use every single day and part of your life. We will look into how body language reading can be used in every aspect of our daily lives.

First, let's think about when we wake up. Typically, when we wake up, we get ready for the day and eat breakfast. Often, these events may take place surrounded by your family or by roommates. Mornings can be a difficult time for many people, so it is important to be able to read the body language of the people around us during this time.

In the morning, if people are yawning, it means that they are still tired. If they are avoiding eye contact or walking around with their shoulders hunched inward, it may mean that they are not yet ready to talk to you or the other people in the home.

If they make eye contact and smile, they may want to talk before leaving the house for the day. They may want to catch up over breakfast or simply say good morning.

If a family member is jittery or unhappy in the morning, they might be nervous about something they need to do that day. If you know they have a big test or presentation coming up, wish them luck and tell them you know that they will do a great job. If you are not sure what they are nervous about, consider asking them. They may need your support before they take on their big task of the day.

Let us consider your commute to work. This seems like an odd time to have to read body language, but occasionally you will want to read the body language of the people driving near you. For example, a friend of mine told me this story: they had miscalculated a lane change on their way to work one day. When he realized that he had accidentally cut off the other car, he rolled his window down and apologetically waved to the other car. Sure enough, both cars ended up side by side. The other driver acknowledged the apology with a wave though she didn't seem too pleased with what had happened. In this example, my friend managed to right the wrong though the other driver's facial expression made it evident that they hadn't appreciated the incident.

Consider a deeper analysis of your workday. Given the fact that we devote a considerable amount of time to work, it is important to use body language skills smartly while you are at work. You will probably want your body language to portray you as a successful and confident person. Try drinking your morning coffee before you enter the door so that you do not enter the building while you are still yawning. If you arrive at work focused and energetic, you will seem passionate to the people around you.

You will also want your coworkers to see you as confident so that they know you are capable of success. This will help them trust you with your tasks and even look up to you as a role model. To do this, consider using power stances and power body language.

There is nothing like a good handshake to click with someone who is not feeling their best. This is highly effective, especially in early morning meetings, since not everything is a morning person. Positive energy can certainly be contagious.

However, it is important to be sincere about your confidence to not give off "fake" confidence. This is why I take time to pay attention to my interactions with colleagues and customers. One such exercise that I do is to pay attention to video calls. During a video call, I can see my face while I am speaking with my interlocutor. This allows me to see my facial expressions and analyze my reactions when speaking. This is one of the few times in which you can gain a third-party perspective on how you communicate with others.

It is equally as important to be able to read the body language of your coworkers. If a coworker is upset with you, they may not express it verbally because it may not be an appropriate conversation to have in a work setting. If you can discover this through their body language early on in the situation, you might be able to turn the negative feelings around right away.

If a person is stressed at work, they might need help with their tasks. If they are embarrassed by this, they may not ask for help. If you can read their body language in these situations, you may be able to help them and avoid having them make a mistake for the company.

I recall one occasion some years ago in one of the first jobs I had. There was a new colleague who was very shy and extremely uncomfortable during their first week. I could tell they were struggling with some tasks but couldn't work up the courage to ask for help. I could tell they needed help by the drooping shoulders and low head position when going over files. So, I walked over and offered my help. They immediately accepted. It turned out that it wasn't anything major, but this colleague simply needed some pointers in the right direction. This was one of the first interactions in which I felt satisfied that I had gotten the right reading on a person.

Another important part of your day would be the commute home. During this time, you would want to use body language in the same way you used it on your way into work. This is especially important if you happen to see the same folks day in and day out. It is a way of making life just a bit more pleasant for others on your way home.

Once you get home, body language is again important with your family. Even if you are tired from a long day at work, you will want to make sure that your body language stays positive so that your family members can see that you love them and are excited to be home with them for the evening.

You will also need to read their body language during this time. If a family member seems sad through the movements of their body, they may have had a hard day. If they are slouching, looking at the ground, and not smiling, you may want to ask them what is wrong. They may need you to listen and help them through a difficult thing that happened to them during their day at work or school.

You will even want to use your ability to read body language to care for your young children if you have them. If your young child is yawning and acting as if they are tired even though it is not yet bed-time, you may want to consider putting them down for the night at an earlier than usual time to ensure that they get the rest that they need.

When it comes to your relationship with your husband or wife, you want to make sure that their body language is positive as well. If it is not, ask them what is wrong. Spend some time working on your re-lationship by talking or even cuddling to show that you love each other. This body language and touch can benefit your relationship and day-to-day life in many ways.

These are ways that you may use body language on a typical day, but we know that most days are far from typical. Usually, you will have extra events that you need to attend outside of your normal com-mitments. We will look into how you can use your ability to read body language in a couple of these situations.

For example, some nights you may go out to dinner with friends instead of eating at home. This can be a fun way to catch up with the people you do not see daily. At dinner, you should be aware of your body language and the body language of the people around you. You will want to make sure that you are smiling and making eye contact to show that you are interested in what your friends have to say and that you are happy that you have the chance to spend time with them. You will want to avoid signs that show you are tired as these can make your friends think that you would rather be at home resting than spending time with them. Even if this is true, you do not want your friends to believe it!

You will also want to read the body language of the friends you are having dinner with. When you talk to them, make sure that they are remaining happy and are not upset by anything you say. Pay attention to if they are making eye contact and smiling to ensure that they are having a good time as well.

One classic example, in this case, is salespeople. Effective sales professionals can make eye contact with their customers in a friendly, non-threatening way while using their hands and facial expressions to ensure an inviting atmosphere. Also, they can use their tone of voice so that customers feel comfortable rather than pushed around. Indeed, effective salespeople are excellent communicators at all levels.

Another thing that you may do that is out of the ordinary during a day is going to a doctor's appointment. You may want to make sure that your body language does not show that you are nervous at this appointment. It is okay to be nervous, but if you do not want the people around you to know how you feel, you may want to remember to make eye contact and try not to fidget with your hands.

Lastly, it is worth mentioning that your ability to put nonverbal communication to good use will allow you to communicate with others on a much deeper level. This leads to more meaningful relationships in which you can connect with people on a very personal and relatable level. This is what sets remarkable people apart from the rest. When you can connect with people at a very personal level, you will become the type of person that everyone will want to be around. That will not only increase your chances of getting what you want out of life, but it will also help you build up your self-confidence in such a way that you can be truly proud of yourself.

That alone is worth far more than any material possession.

Chapter 13:
How to Control Your Body Language

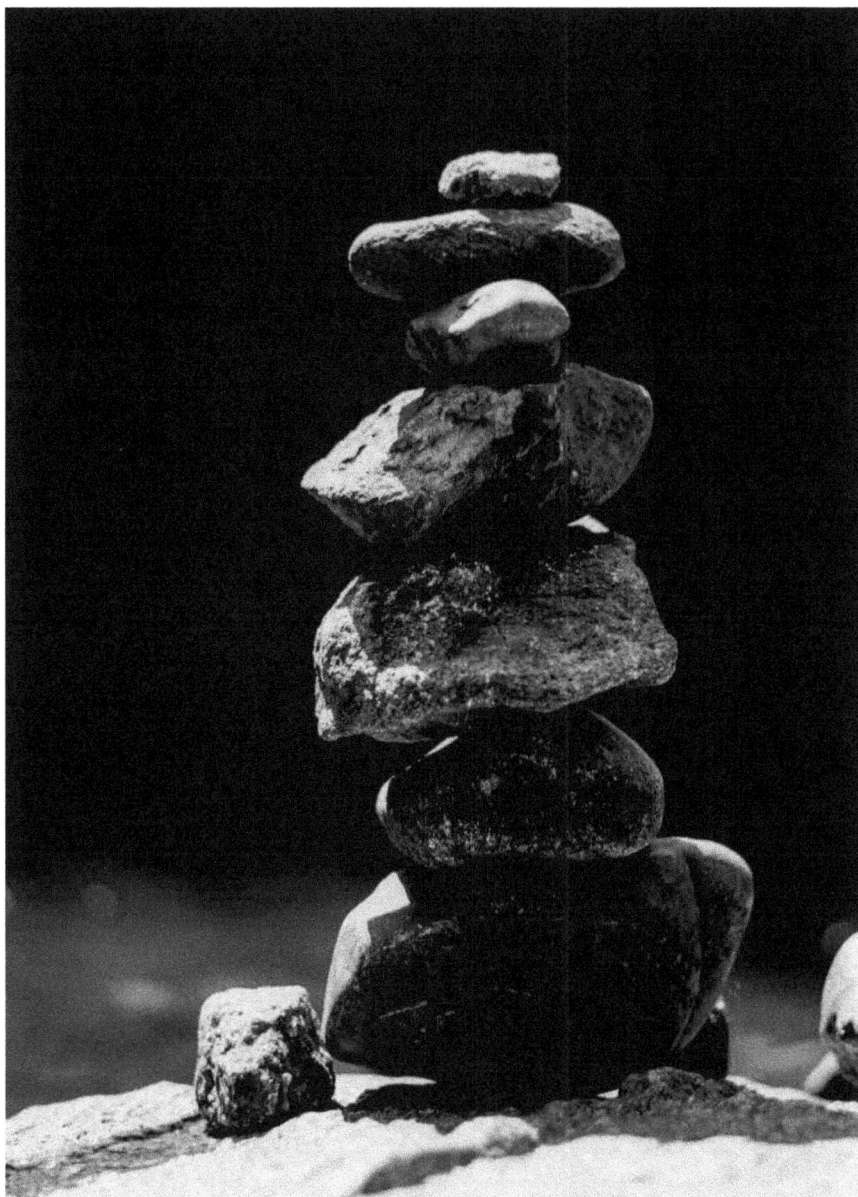

Body language can enhance your communication skills in a great way. You can have effective communication skills only if you can control your body language. Before, we look at the most used body language for manipulation. It is important to know how to take charge of your body. Can we base these on the quote that, 'Charity begins at home?' Yeah, you cannot have an interest in understanding how to manipulate other people positively, yet you do not know how to take control of yourself. Let us kick off with understanding and having control of our body language.

How to Take Control and Manipulate Your Body Language

Research has shown that when you are aware of the happenings of your body, you can manipulate it by training yourself to have control and even mold it to have effective communication. Further research recommends that you take some breathing exercises before going into a meeting or presentation. It will help you be calm and take note of your posture and gestures while on presentation. As you have noted by now, mirroring is a good technique. Always try to be keen on what the next person is doing nonverbally and copy that. It will help you become more effective in your communication with them. They will understand you better because this tunes your mind to the ability to communicate more truthfully at a place of relaxation.

However, you should be careful while shaping your body language. This is to ensure that the body language that you portray matches what you are trying to present. A mismatch may bring confusion and may not be relevant at the moment. The person you are in conversation with may mistake you for meaning something else contrary to what you intended. The secret to having control of your body language is to take your time to learn it, to be aware of your nonverbal cues as you apply what you learn.

The Body Language That Will Help You Take Charge of Your Space

Effective management involves individuals being able to encourage and have a positive influence. In planning for an important appointment, maybe with your employees, management team, or partners, you focus on what to say, memorizing critical points, and rehearsing your presentation to make you feel believable and persuasive. This is something you should be aware of, of course.

Here is what you should know if you want to take control of your position, at work, at a presentation, or as a leader.

Seven Seconds is What You Have to Make an Impression

First impressions are essential in market relationships. When somebody psychologically marks you as trustworthy, or skeptical, strong, or submissive, you will be seen through such a filter in any other dealings that you may have with that person. Your partners will look for the finest in you if they like you. They will suspect all of your deeds if they distrust you. While you can't stop people from having quick decisions, as a defense mechanism, the human mind is programmed in this way; you can learn how to make these choices effective for you. In much less than seven seconds, the initial perceptions are developed and strongly influenced by body language. Studies have found that nonverbal signals have more than four times the effect on the first impression you create than you speak. These are what you should know regarding making positive and lasting first impressions:

- Start by changing your attitude. People immediately pick up your mood. Have you noticed that you immediately get turned off after finding a customer service representative who has a negative attitude? You feel like leaving or request to be served by a different person. That will happen to you too if you have a bad attitude, which is highly noticeable. Think of the situation and make a deliberate decision about the mindset you want to represent before you meet a client, or join the meeting room for a company meeting, or step on the scene to make an analysis.
- Smile. Smiling is a good sign that leaders are under using. A smile is a message, a gesture of recognition and acceptance. "I'm friendly and accessible," it says. Having a smile on your face will change the mood of your audience. If they had another perception of you, a smile can change that and make them relax.
- Make contact with your eyes. Looking at somebody's eyes conveys vitality and expresses interest and transparency. A nice way to help you make eye contact is to practice observing the eye color of everybody you encounter to enhance your eye contact. Overcome being shy and practice this great body language.
- Lean in gently. The body language that has you leaning forward often expresses that you are actively participating and interested in the discussion. But be careful about the space of the other individual. This means staying about two ft away in most professional situations.
- Shaking hands. This will be the best way to develop a relationship. It's the most successful as well. Research indicates that maintaining the very same degree of partnership you can get with a simple handshake takes a minimum of three hours of intense communication. You should ensure that you have palm-to-palm touch and also that your hold is firm but not bone-crushing.

- Look at your position. Studies have found that the unique-ness of posture, presenting yourself in a way that exposes your openness and takes up space, generates a sense of control that creates behavior changes in a subject independent of its specific rank or function in an organization. In fact, in three studies, it was repeatedly found that body position was more important than the hierarchical structure in making a person think, act, and be viewed more strongly.
- Building your credibility is dependent on how you align your nonverbal communication. Using an electroencephalograph (EEG) device to calculate "event-related potentials"–brain waves that shape peaks and valleys to examine gesture effects prove that one of these valleys happens when movements that dispute what is spoken are shown to subjects. This is the same dip in the brainwave that occurs when people listen to a language that does not make sense. In a rather reasonable way, they simply do not make sense if leaders say one thing and their behaviors point to something else. Each time your facial expressions do not suit your words, for example, losing eye contact or looking all over the room when trying to express candor, swaying back on the heels while thinking about the company's bright future, or locking arms around the chest when announcing transparency. All this causes the verbal message to disappear.

What your hands mean when you use them

Have you at any point seen that when individuals are energetic about what they're stating, their signals naturally turned out to be increasingly energized? Their hands and arms constantly move, accentuating focus and passing on eagerness.

You might not have known about this association previously; however, you intuitively felt it. Research shows that an audience will generally view individuals who utilize a more prominent assortment of hand motions in a progressively ideal light. Studies likewise find that individuals who convey through dynamic motioning will, in general, be assessed as warm, pleasant, and vivacious. In contrast, the individuals who stay still or whose motions appear to be mechanical or "wooden" are viewed as legitimate, cold, and systematic.

That is one motivation behind why signals are so basic to a pioneer's viability and why getting them directly in an introduction associates so effectively with a group of people. You may have seen senior administrators commit little avoidable errors. At the point when pioneers don't utilize motions accurately on the off chance that they let their hands hang flaccidly to the side or fasten their hands before their bodies in the exemplary "fig leaf" position, it recommends they have no passionate interest in the issues or are not persuaded about the fact of the matter they're attempting to make.

To utilize signals adequately, pioneers should know how those developments will, in all probability, be seen. Here are four basic hand motions and the messages behind them:

- Concealed hands- Shrouded hands to make you look less reliable. This is one of the nonverbal signs that is profoundly imbued in our subliminal. Our precursors settled on endurance choices dependent on bits of visual data they grabbed from each other. In ancient times, when somebody drew nearer with hands out of view, it was a sign of potential peril. Albeit today the risk of shrouded hands is more representative than genuine, our instilled mental warnings remain.

- Blame game- I've frequently observed officials utilize this signal in gatherings, arrangements, or meetings for accentuation or to show strength. The issue is that forceful blame dispensing can recommend that the pioneer is losing control of the circumstance. The signal bears a resemblance to parental reprimanding or play area harassing.

- Eager gestures- There is an intriguing condition of the hand and arm development with vitality. If you need to extend more excitement and drive, you can do as such by expanded motioning. Over-motioning (particularly when hands are raised over the shoulders) can cause you to seem whimsical, less trustworthy, and less incredible.
- Laidback gestures—Arms held at midsection tallness and motions inside that level plane help you—and the group of spectators—feel focused and formed. Arms at the midsection and bowed to a 45-degree point (joined by a position about shoulder-width wide) will likewise assist you with keeping grounded, empowered, and centered.

In this quick-paced, techno-charged time of email, writings, video chats, and video visits, one generally accepted fact remain: Face-to-confront is the most liked, gainful, and amazing correspondence medium. The more business pioneers convey electronically, all the more squeezing turns into the requirement for individual communication.

Here's the reason:

In face to face gatherings, our brain processes the nonstop course of nonverbal signs that we use as the reason for building trust and expert closeness. Eye to eye collaboration is data-rich. We translate what individuals state to us just halfway from the words they use. We get a large portion of the message (and most emotional subtlety behind the words) from vocal tone, pacing, outward appearances, and other nonverbal signs. What's more, we depend on prompt input on others' quick reactions to assist us with checking how well our thoughts are being acknowledged.

So strong is the nonverbal connection between people that, when we are in certified affinity with somebody, we subliminally coordinate our body positions, developments, and even our breathing rhythms with theirs. Most intriguing, in up close and personal experiences, the mind's "reflect neurons" impersonate practices, yet sensations and sentiments too. When we are denied these relational prompts and are compelled to depend on the printed or verbally expressed word alone, the cerebrum battles and genuine correspondence endures.

Chapter 14:
Body Language Mistakes to Avoid

In a business setting, you must also avoid various types of body language mistakes simply because using specific body language gestures can sabotage your career.

Some of these mistakes include:

Exaggerated gestures

When talking to people, avoid using exaggerated gestures because using such gestures may imply you're overstretching the truth or trying to hide dishonesty. To show honesty and confidence, use small and controlled gestures.

Don't look at Your Wristwatch

Looking at your wristwatch, especially when you do it consistently, is a sign of complete disrespect interpreted to mean you aren't interested in the conversation or find the current conversation boring. It could also make you seem an impatient person.

Don't look at the Door

Don't constantly glance at the door and completely avoid looking at the door except, of course, when the conversation is over and you'd like to take your leave.

Don't Turn Away from Others

People interpret turning away from them as rudeness or a sign of discomfort. Turning away could also make it seem as if you're uninterested in the conversation or you don't trust the person speaking.

Don't Cross Your Arms or Legs

As stated earlier, crossing your arms and legs is a closed body language. Crossed body language isn't good for business. When you display closed body language, business associates may interpret it to mean you are being dishonest, hiding something, or deliberately shutting the other person out. Crossing your arms and legs could also signify stubbornness or defiance.

Being too Pedantic

Body language needs to be used naturally, or else others will think you are hiding something, or you are just irritatingly happy or good-willed. If you are trying to sell something or intimidate people with your body language, don't be surprised if they notice what you are doing. Hand gestures should be used sparingly and should not risk hitting other people in the face. Your posture doesn't always have to be perfect so that you look like a soldier on parade.

Lacking Assertiveness

Assertive might not be the correct word here, but it lets you know how you need to behave more than the vague idea of 'not being confident.' You need to avoid defaulting to being too submissive when you are questioned or speaking to someone you need to connect with. This can mean making sure you maintain eye contact and only breaking it by looking to the side and not glancing down. It can mean being willing to question others when you think something isn't right and directing the topic of a conversation.

World Dominance

If you are dealing with someone more reserved, quiet, nervous, or perhaps not very confident in themselves, you should adapt to that. These people will generally want space and lower-energy body language from you. This means not getting too close, not putting pressure on them to speak up, and not being open with your body to the point of putting them on edge.

Reading this can be difficult at first, and you will need to learn how to match energy levels with other people. Mirroring and matching, and reading other people through baselines will help you a lot in this regard.

Knowing your place in a social hierarchy is important as well. If you try to be too assertive towards your superior, or even just an elder, this can lead them into thinking you are disrespectful and arrogant. This might not always be as obvious as it first appears either. You might technically outrank the office secretary, but if they have been with the business a long time, you will want to show them respect as they may have more power than you in certain matters despite the fact you 'outrank' them in the office hierarchy.

Insensitivity

Following on from the last mistake, being insensitive to the feelings and norms of the place you are in is often a big mistake when it comes to body language. In most cases, if you are being insensitive with your body language, it's because you aren't sensitive with your thoughts and communication. However, sometimes you might have your arms crossed across your chest because you are cold or find it comfortable. So make sure you pay attention to what you are doing when it matters most. There is a learning curve in certain situations, and it can be steep. If you've never had to care for an injured person before, it is difficult to make sure you are using the right kind of comforting body language.

Inconsistent Facial Expression is bad

Your words and tone of voice should match your facial expressions. You cannot be speaking strongly and passionately, expressing displeasure, and at the same time, smiling. This sort of inconsistency will send the wrong message and may end up confusing your addressee.

Avoid heavy nods

Heavy nodes make you appear as if you're feigning an understanding of the topic in discussion. Although nodding is a sign of agreement of concentration on the discussion, avoid heavy nods. Whenever you don't understand something, rather than a nod, ask directly related questions because of questions. Questions make you appear attentive and interested. If you don't understand something, ask the other party for clarification.

Avoid clenching your fists

The clenched fist is a form of closed body language that makes you seem defensive and argumentative.

Don't get too close

Respect people's personal spaces and avoid getting too close to them except if you already have a personal relationship with the person you're engaging in conversation or discussion.

Conclusion

If your mind is reeling from all the information shared so far, brace yourself. You see, this is an exceedingly vast topic. It is an essential topic because communication is one of the essential parts of our lives. How we communicate impacts our relationships, whether private, personal, or professional.

As with anything else, the impact can be positive or negative, so knowing what your body is saying on your behalf is of the utmost importance. It is in understanding that there is so much to know and that you can learn it over time by paying attention and putting in some effort.

Imagine that you are a very shy person who has amazing ideas for inventions or songs or movies, or whatever. Now, imagine how hard it would be for a very timid person to get those great ideas across to the right patent attorney, the right musician, or the right producer if they could barely speak above a whisper when they were nervous.

If they finally do get a meeting with their target audience, how would it look if they averted their eyes and crossed their arms over their body the whole time? Do you think they would be taken seriously? What is the possibility that they would win an influential person in a position of influence over under those circumstances?

There is nothing wrong with any personality type, but if you have a timid personality, know what your body language is saying on your behalf. If that is not what you want to convey, you can learn better behaviors that reflect what you want to say.

What of the person who is the opposite? What if you were naturally loud, bordering on boisterous, and the more nervous you became, the louder you seemed to get?

Being aware of how your volume affects others, you might try to tone it down a bit, but those who are naturally boisterous tend to have "big" body language as well.

If you walk into a room and begin to grip and shake hands as if you were arm wrestling, you would naturally start your event with mistrust and wariness about your motives though you said very little at a modified decibel.

Here is one last word of caution about becoming a student of body language; never use one cue to determine what a speaker means. Several factors are involved in each person's dynamic, and all must be considered before making an important determination.

Factors that could affect someone's body language might include a physical or mental disability or limitation, a person's culture or background, or even a current health crisis.

Be aware that you can be influenced by body language with or without your consent, and you can influence others by your body language, whether you are aware of it or even whether or not you mean to.

Body language is a powerful tool. Understand it and that understanding thoughtfully.